THE COMPLETE SYSTEM FOR EQUIPPING LEADERS & MOBILIZING MINISTRY TEAMS

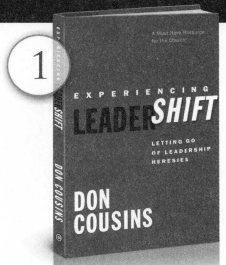

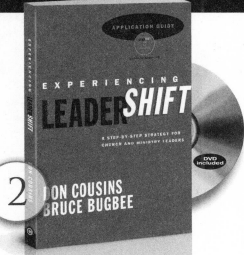

FOR PASTORS AND LEADERS

① Experiencing LeaderShift—Applicable for leaders and anyone who wants to participate fully as a member of the body of Christ, this book offers insights into destructive heresies leaders have mistakenly embraced and explains the biblical foundation for leading as God intended.

② Experiencing LeaderShift Application Guide—Designed to help turn the vision from *Experiencing LeaderShift* into action, this guide instructs ministry leaders how to better equip others to function as devoted members of the body of Christ. This dynamic guide includes a six-session DVD.

FOR MINISTRY LEADERS AND THEIR TEAMS

③ Experiencing LeaderShift Together—Aimed at mobilizing church staff, volunteers, and church-ministry team members, these comprehensive guides describe God's plan for His church and the roles of its members. Together, leaders and participants will learn specifically how their efforts can transform their ministry within the body of Christ.

What people are saying about ...

E X P E R I E N C I N G

LEADER*SHIFT*
TOGETHER

"The best thing about *Experiencing LeaderShift* is that it's so practical. It's like somebody finally put the wheels on the leadership-development car. I use it at every level of ministry, whether I'm working with our elder board, staff, or unpaid ministry team leaders. We definitely believe that we're all in this together, working as a team to equip others for ministry."

Tom Cramer, associate pastor Geneva Presbyterian Church, Laguna Hills, California

"Two things I especially like about *Experiencing LeaderShift*: First, our experienced leaders started thinking outside the box, developed new enthusiasm for their responsibilities, and began to see a better picture of where their ministry fit into the overall scheme of things. Second, this training provides an entirely new way to view and do ministry that alleviates the anxiety inexperienced ministry leaders often have. In the place of that fear, a new energy develops to take on the challenge. You can see it in their countenance, hear it in their voices, and find it in their team members. Now ministry becomes contagious and energizes all who participate."

Dave Carder, assistant pastor of First Evangelical Free Church, Fullerton, California

"*Experiencing LeaderShift* is food for the mind and inspiration for the soul in helping us understand how the church can and should function.... No stone is left unturned, and ministry is broken down and then rebuilt in the model that produces spiritual fruit from our church ministries, its leaders, and the ministry servants who are mentored. In the end God is brought positive attention (glory) and the people of the church are built up!"

Barry Carroll, executive pastor of Horizon Christian Church, Valrico, Florida

"The spiritual growth of God's people is not dependent on the leadership practices of corporate America, or the polity of our church, or having the intimacy of a small congregation or even the resources of a large church. True spiritual growth emerges as we practically implement the thoughts and practices of Jesus in the body of Christ.... *Experiencing LeaderShift* has been instrumental in changing everything from the way we approach volunteer leadership to staff hiring. Matching spiritual gifts to the role needing to be filled has energized the body to function supernaturally."

Erich Roeh, executive pastor of Neighborhood Church of Redding, California

"My encounter with *Experiencing LeaderShift* took the *idea* of becoming an equipping church from a conceptual model to a practical reality. *LeaderShift* gave me practical handles for recognizing and empowering ministry leaders to meaningfully equip their teams. As equipping leaders, our role is to provide the environments, teaching, opportunities, and vehicles to allow people to keep all the gears turning in harmony. *LeaderShift* provides the framework and the applications to train, release, and envision your ministry leaders to join the Holy Spirit in truly fruitful and fulfilling ministry. As one of the pastors on our staff put it, 'I've had years of education, and over fifteen years of pastoral experience—and this is the first time I've ever understood equipping leadership with such clarity.'"

Shawn Andrews, ministry pastor at Daybreak Church, Pennsylvania

"Early on in my discipleship journey, *my way* of doing ministry looked a lot different from the way *Jesus* did ministry. Now, thirteen years later, my way is finally *shifting* to His. *Experiencing LeaderShift* has been a transforming process. In part, I see *LeaderShift* as a call for the church to pray about being intentional about discipleship. Jesus prayed and intentionally poured his life into others. He has been and will always be the perfect example of how we carry out the Great Commission."

Scott Bircher, Saturday night worship arts coordinator at Covenant United Methodist Church, Greenville, North Carolina

EXPERIENCING
LEADER*SHIFT*
TOGETHER

EXPERIENCING
LEADER*SHIFT*
TOGETHER

A STEP-BY-STEP STRATEGY FOR
SMALL GROUPS AND MINISTRY TEAMS

DON COUSINS
BRUCE BUGBEE

transforming lives together

EXPERIENCING LEADERSHIFT TOGETHER LEADER'S GUIDE
Published by David C. Cook
4050 Lee Vance View
Colorado Springs, CO 80918 U.S.A.

David C. Cook Distribution Canada
55 Woodslee Avenue, Paris, Ontario, Canada N3L 3E5

David C. Cook U.K., Kingsway Communications
Eastbourne, East Sussex BN23 6NT, England

David C. Cook and the graphic circle C logo
are registered trademarks of Cook Communications Ministries.

The Web site addresses recommended throughout this book are offered as a resource to you. These Web sites are not intended in any way to be or imply an endorsement on the part of David C. Cook, nor do we vouch for their content.

Unless otherwise indicated, Scripture quotations are from the *New American Standard Bible* © 1960, 1995 by The Lockman Foundation. Used by permission. Scripture quotations marked NKJV are taken from the New King James Version. Copyright © 1982 by Thomas Nelson, Inc. Used by permission. All rights reserved. Italics in Scripture quotations are the authors' emphasis.

ISBN 978-1-4347-6812-4

© 2008 Don Cousins and Bruce Bugbee
Published in association with the Literary agency of Wolgemuth & Associates, Inc.

The Team: Terry Behimer, Thomas Womack, Amy Kiechlin, Jaci Schneider, and Karen Athen
Cover Design: The DesignWorks Group, David Uttley
Interior Design: The DesignWorks Group

Printed in the United States of America
First Edition 2008

1 2 3 4 5 6 7 8 9 10

051608

CONTENTS

FOR LEADERS ONLY

GETTING STARTED

Welcome to *Experiencing LeaderShift Together.*

By now you know you're called by God to equip others for the work of service. How do you fulfill this challenge?

That's what the *Experiencing LeaderShift* system is primarily about—helping you function as an equipping leader.

The system includes three resources:

- The book *Experiencing LeaderShift* helps you capture a vision for biblical leadership.
- The second resource, the *Experiencing LeaderShift Application Guide,* takes you through the equipping process—calling, connecting, coaching, and changing. To the degree that you follow this process with others, you'll do a fantastic job of equipping them. Instead of trying to do the work of ten people, you'll train ten people (and probably many more) to do that work.
- Now you've moved on to *Experiencing LeaderShift Together,* the third resource in the system, and one that's specifically designed to assist you in equipping those who follow you as part of a ministry team or small group. As you lead them through this study, you'll be making a deposit into their lives that will reap dividends for eternity.

This Leader's Guide for *Experiencing LeaderShift Together* has been developed and designed for you to help maximize the impact of this study in the lives of your members. Our hope is to provide you here with everything you'll need to lead this study successfully.

While some preparation time will be required, it doesn't need to be extensive; we want you to focus instead on spending time with those you lead.

There's also a separate Participant's Guide for *Experiencing LeaderShift Together.* **It's very important**

that each of your members has his or her own copy. This is where your members will take notes, follow along as the session unfolds, complete assessments, and find daily devotionals.

SESSION OPTIONS

The content in this Leader's Guide is arranged in six sessions (plus an optional introductory session, which we strongly encourage you to start with).

You have three basic options for how these six sessions can unfold:

- **Option 1:** The Six-Pack—six regular sessions (plus an introductory session), each about forty-five to fifty minutes in length.

    That's the minimum these sessions are designed for.

- **Option 2:** The Six-Pack Plus—six regular sessions (plus an introductory session), each lasting one and a half to two hours.

    Option 2 will be more beneficial than Option 1. And this Leader's Guide contains plenty of content to expand each session to two hours.

- **Option 3:** The Twelve-Pack—expanding the course to twelve to eighteen sessions. In this case, each session becomes two or three sessions of forty-five to fifty minutes in length.

    Option 3 provides the most benefit. Again, the book has plenty of content to do this.

So how do you determine which of these options is best for you and your members?

Here are six factors to consider:

1. *Time availability.* Realistically, how much time can everyone in your group commit to each session?

2. *Content value.* At this particular time in the life of your small group or ministry team, how valuable is this content for them? If it's exactly what they currently need, it won't be wise to rush through it. Remember, you're laying a foundation for their participation in the body of Christ that will serve these believers for a lifetime— even an eternity.

3. *Scripture emphasis.* How much time do you want to allow for walking through the Bible passages in each session? Some key passages support each session's content.

4. *Time for discussion.* How extensive do you want your discussion time to be? Considering your members, will the discussion be only surface-level if time is too short? Will you want to give everyone the opportunity to respond in-depth? (Plenty of questions are provided in this guide to fill up the extended session times.)

5. *Level of interaction.* How open and comfortable are your members with one another? How talkative are they? Would they be frustrated if you have to cut off their discussion?

6. *Application emphasis.* How much time do you want to devote in the sessions to the assessments and personal application segments? Should you spend some time completing the assessments or assignments while you're all together? Or will you plan on always doing these as outside assignments?

Consider all these factors as you look over this Leader's Guide; then decide on the option that's right for you.

Once you make your decision, schedule your meetings at the pace that works best for your members. We suggest you meet no less than once a month—taking longer than that between sessions will hinder continuity. The optimum pace would be weekly or biweekly. That gives everyone enough time to complete assessments and assignments, while also giving you opportunity for personal follow-up with individuals.

GROUP RELATIONAL DYNAMICS

Group/Team Size

The number of participants will impact the way you lead these sessions. A typical small group has six to twelve members, but if you're taking a ministry team through this study, it might include a significantly larger number.

If the number of participants is large, some segments of each session will work better if you divide into smaller groups. Think this through ahead of time to maximize the benefit for all involved.

The DVD

The DVD included with this Leader's Guide begins with a segment titled "For Leaders," followed by the teaching segment for each of the six sessions.

We strongly encourage you to watch all seven of these DVD segments on your own before getting together with everyone for the first session. This will give you a clear understanding of the content and flow of *Experiencing LeaderShift Together*.

Participation and Application

Active participation from everyone is extremely important as you meet together. Your job as the leader is to discern and remove any obstacles that may be holding someone back from taking an active part in the discussions.

It's also your responsibility as the leader to emphasize personal application of the truths that are learned and discussed in each session. Remember: True-life change comes with *application*, not information.

You have a tremendous opportunity in the weeks ahead as you join others in *Experiencing LeaderShift Together*. We believe this will be a life-altering experience for many as they find their place of passion and giftedness in God's family, among their brothers and sisters in Christ.

MINISTRY TEAM ... OR SMALL GROUP?

While *Experiencing LeaderShift Together* is designed for both ministry teams and small groups, we want to make it clear we see a difference between the two.

We define a **ministry team** as *a group of people who all serve in the same ministry.* It could be the children's ministry, youth ministry, prayer ministry, music ministry, or any other. This ministry team may be four in number or forty.

We define a **small group** as *a gathering of people (usually six to twelve in number) who meet regularly to encourage one another in their spiritual journeys, but who serve in a variety of ministries.* One person in your group may be involved in children's ministry, another in youth ministry, another in the worship ministry, and so on. To repeat, if the people in your group are serving in *different* ministries, then you fit our classification as a small group.

For Leaders of Ministry Teams

Again, a ministry team is simply a group of people serving together in the same ministry.

If that describes the people you're leading through *Experiencing LeaderShift Together,* the number of participants will obviously affect the way you structure the sessions. If it's only four, you can do everything in this study together as an entire team. If it's forty, you'll need to break down into smaller groups for discussion and interaction. You may even want to consider dividing into a few smaller groups that meet at different times.

In both the participant's and leader's guide, you'll notice a special section in each session titled "For Ministry Teams." Here we've included additional discussion questions that apply *specifically to ministry teams.* Use some or all of these based on your objectives and the time you have available.

For ministry teams in particular, it's especially important to allow for enough time together to maximize the impact of this study. Consider carefully the likely value of the Six-Pack Plus Option (two-hour sessions) for your team, as well as the possibility of the Twelve-Pack Option (twelve to eighteen sessions of forty-five to fifty minutes).

However you decide to structure the gathering of your team to study *Experiencing LeaderShift Together,* the following objectives should be in the forefront of your mind:

1. See to it that all the people on your team are serving in "the zone of God's anointing." Are they in a role that fits who God made them to be?

2. Ensure that the entire team understands what each other does. It's not just "What do *I* do?" but also "What do *you* do?" Help them be aware of each other's contributions to the ministry.

3. This is a biggie: Help your team members relate to one another as *teammates,* not merely as participants in a group. Through this study, you'll want to take significant strides in functioning well as a team. Be alert to learn how you can do this.

The bottom line: Your overarching goal is to equip every member of your ministry team for "success" as God defines it:

—Being Faithful

—Bearing Fruit

—Experiencing Fulfillment

—Making God Famous

For Leaders of Small Groups

Again, we define a "small group" as a gathering of people (usually six to twelve in number) who meet regularly for spiritual encouragement, but who serve in a variety of ministries (rather than all on the same ministry team).

If this describes your context for studying *Experiencing LeaderShift Together,* then as a small group leader, keep in mind these primary objectives:

1. Help all the members of your group discover personally "the zone of God's anointing." You'll want to affirm them in their spiritual gifts, encourage them in discerning where their God-given passion lies, and help them realize where God manifests Himself through their life in service to others.

2. Help them find a place of service in the body of Christ that reflects their zone of anointing. Through this study, you want to help them be successful according to how God defines success:

—Being Faithful

—Bearing Fruit

—Experiencing Fulfillment

—Making God Famous

3. Help all your members become people of influence within the ministry where they serve. They may need direction and assistance in taking what they learn in this study to the ministry leader they serve under. You might encourage them to show their ministry leader the book *Experiencing LeaderShift,* as well as the *Experiencing LeaderShift Application Guide,* as a way to encourage and serve their leader.

Note: We encourage you to contact the leader of each ministry in which your group members serve. Tell these leaders what this study is all about. If a leader isn't familiar with the *Experiencing LeaderShift* system, this would be a good time to share what you've gained personally by your use of it.

SESSION STRUCTURE

Below we'll outline how the content is structured in each of the six numbered sessions in *Experiencing LeaderShift Together*. But first, we want to encourage you to hold an introductory session with your group. We've included a suggested plan for it in this Leader's Guide. During this introductory session, you can distribute copies of the Participant's Guide to everyone, gain a clearer understanding of the group's current ministry involvement, and cast a vision for what lies ahead.

For the other six sessions in this Leader's Guide, here's what you'll find. All of these follow the same three-part structure:

> **Part 1—For the Leader**—This includes specific information for you as the leader, including session *objectives, icebreaker* ideas, and suggestions for *prayer together.*

> **Part 2—Learning Together**—The content in this part also appears in the Participant's Guide. (Any special instructions for you as the leader will be printed in **bold**.) Here you'll find the basic step-by-step flow of the teaching and discussion in each week's session. These steps include each session's *introduction, warm-up questions, DVD teaching,* a *key Bible passage, discussion questions,* and a special focus *for ministry teams.*

> **Part 3—Application Zone**—This part's content is also included in the Participant's Guide. (Again, any special leader's instructions are printed in **bold**.) This part includes the all-important *application* or *assessment* content for each session, along with *Scripture memory* suggestions plus *daily devotions* for your members' use on their own in the coming week.

This structure for each session is intended to help you, the leader, succeed in your role. To understand it well (which is critically important), read carefully through the following explanations of each part.

Part 1—For the Leader

The content in this part of each session is *not* included in the Participant's Guide. It's just for you as the leader.

Each session begins with a short explanation of how that session connects with the book *Experiencing LeaderShift*. Then you'll find a list of the *objectives* for the session, some *icebreaker* suggestions, and possible guidelines for *prayer together*.

Objectives

You'll find a clear articulation of the objectives for each session. These are here because, to state the obvious, you need to know where you're going.

Consider the importance of a hunter having a target. The finest equipment money can buy, plus all the practice in the world, would mean nothing without a target. Or consider an athlete who doesn't understand the criteria for winning. It would be pointless for him or her to even enter the competition.

In the same way, be clear about what it is you're seeking to accomplish in each session. Read and reread the session objectives so you know exactly where you're heading.

Icebreaker

The icebreaker is a welcome of sorts, and it's intended to serve two purposes:

1. To help all the members transition, in their thoughts and attention, to your time together and what it's all about. You want to help them move mentally from "wherever they've been" to "where they are now."

2. To help them reconnect with each other emotionally and spiritually. Feeling secure and comfortable with one another from the start will make healthy interaction easier throughout the session.

We'll take a look in the next section at suggested icebreaker questions and activities. But first, some important points to remember:

*   The icebreaker is *optional*. You may not need it at all. (You may decide that the session's *Introduction* plus the *Warm-up*—both of which are described below—will provide all the transition and reconnection your group needs.)

*   The icebreaker is *not* the lesson; it's merely a transition to the lesson. So don't spend too much time here. It shouldn't exceed ten minutes in length.

- Icebreaker activities can be humorous or serious. They can have a vertical (spiritual) focus or a horizontal (relational) focus. You may want to vary quite a bit how you approach these each week.

- Some icebreakers will be more effective if done in smaller groups of three or four. Use your own judgment on this.

Prayer Together

We'll leave it up to you to decide how to incorporate prayer into each session. You may want to approach it a little differently each time you meet.

As you begin each session, we encourage you to invite the Father to send forth His Spirit. After all, it's the Holy Spirit who will be the primary teacher and change-agent in your group/team. And God is eager to have His Spirit help you:

> If you then, being evil, know how to give good gifts to your children, how much more will your heavenly Father give the Holy Spirit to those who ask Him? (Luke 11:13)

At times you may want to lead them through a time of prayer using the ACTS acrostic (adoration, confession, thanksgiving, and supplication). Some of this can be done silently, and some aloud.

Another idea: Consider a few rounds of one-sentence prayers. Start with one-sentence *praises,* then one-sentence *thanksgivings,* then one-sentence *intercessions* for one another, etc.

Part 2—Learning Together

Again, the content in this part of each session also appears in the Participant's Guide. (Specific instructions for you as the leader are indicated in **bold** text in this part of each session.)

This part is broken down into the following step-by-step sections:

Introduction

We suggest that you or one of your members read this introduction aloud to help everyone focus on the session's direction.

Warm-up Questions

This is just that—a warm-up. You'll find questions for discussion listed here to help everyone relate to and "feel" what the session is all about.

- Use your judgment as to how many of these warm-up questions you want to use.
- Remember, they're a warm-up to the lesson, not the lesson. Be careful not to spend too much time on these questions—we suggest no more than ten minutes.
- You may find that this warm-up section will sufficiently accomplish the same purpose as the icebreaker ideas. If so, just skip the *Icebreaker* section.

DVD Teaching

As you watch the DVD teaching for each session, everyone can follow along with the outline in the Participant's Guide, which includes an outline of the primary points in the DVD's teaching content.

As they listen, encourage your group members to take notes of anything in the DVD teaching that they consider particularly helpful or significant.

Important: We encourage you, as the leader, to watch *all* the teaching segments *before* your first session. This will be especially valuable in helping you see the path you'll be taking together in the coming weeks.

Key Bible Passage

In each session, we highlight a primary Bible passage that the session's content is based on. The verses are written out in both the Participant's Guide and your Leader's Guide, but the Leader's Guide includes additional notes related to them.

The way you handle this key Bible passage will be determined by the pace of your sessions—which option you chose from the three mentioned in the "Session Options" section previously.

For the *Six-Pack Option,* you'll probably have only enough time to mention the key Bible passage in each session and encourage everyone to read and study it on their own.

For the *Six-Pack Plus Option,* you can quickly walk through the passage, highlighting its key teachings.

If you're following the *Twelve-Pack Option,* take time to read and discuss the passage verse-by-verse, with help from the notes we've provided.

Discussion

The most important time in each session will be your group's discussion of the questions provided in this section.

A few helpful hints:

- For this crucial part of the session, ask the Lord to give you wisdom as you seek to lead your group's discussion.
- It may be helpful to break into smaller groups for this discussion.
- Use as many of the listed questions as time allows. Keeping in mind (1) the objectives for each session, (2) the primary teaching points your members should understand, and (3) the current dynamics in your group/team, choose the questions you believe will be most helpful.

The number and scope of the questions listed here, along with the amount and quality of discussion you anticipate from your members, should be key factors in deciding whether to extend this course to more than six sessions. Plan for as many as needed for maximum value from the study.

For Ministry Teams

Earlier we spelled out what we mean by both "ministry team" and "small group." If your members comprise a ministry team (everyone serving in the same specific ministry), the questions listed in this section will provide additional stimulus for discussion and application.

Use some or all of the questions based on what you want to accomplish, as well as the time available.

Part 3—Application Zone

In this part as well, the content of each session appears in the Participant's Guide, and you'll find specific leader's instructions in **bold** text.

This part has three sections:

Application / Assessment

Some of the sessions have a clear assignment to be completed outside your time together. Session 1, for example, includes a "Spiritual Gift Assessment" and a "Ministry Passion Assessment," which everyone is to complete before they convene for session 2. Make it clear that these assignments aren't optional but are critical to the overall value and application of this study.

Offer whatever assistance you can to help everyone complete the application or assessment.

Scripture Memory

We strongly encourage you to lead your group in memorizing at least one verse connected with each session. We've listed some key verses you can choose from. Or you and your group can pick a verse or two of your own.

Daily Devotions

At the end of each session, we've identified passages that reinforce the content of the session just completed. We've also provided questions to help everyone reflect on what each passage teaches.

We strongly encourage you and your members to utilize these daily devotionals, as they'll reinforce what you're learning, discussing, and applying in each session.

You may want to follow up with your members to see what they're learning from these devotionals.

ICEBREAKER IDEAS

As you prepare for each session, you can refer back to this list for suggested icebreakers.

- Have everyone complete a personal insight statement such as these, using just two or three per session:

  —The highlight of my past week was ...

  —The lowlight of my past week was ...

  —The best thing that happened to me recently is ...

  —The worst thing that happened to me recently is ...

  —I'm really being challenged by ...

  —I'm a bit anxious about ...

  —I'm a bit concerned about ...

  —I would ask you to pray for me concerning ...

  —I'm really looking forward to ...

  —If I could accomplish just one thing in the near future it would be ...

  —I find that I'm really encouraged when ...

  —I find that I'm really discouraged when ...

  —On a scale of one to ten, my week has been a ... (And explain why.)

- Share spiritual growth and discovery. You could ask each person to tell about ...

  —something they found valuable in the previous session.

  —something from their daily devotions.

  —one or two causes for celebration as it relates to God's activity in their life or ministry.

  —one of God's attributes they've experienced recently.

- Encourage and affirm one another. You could ask each person to ...

29

—*share something they appreciate about someone else in the group, such as the person on their right.*

—*choose one or two words that best describe the contribution a group member is making to the team or group.*

—*identify where they can clearly see God's hand upon the life of a group member— where they see God at work in that person's life.*

Also, you can easily come up with your own icebreaker questions and activities that are best suited for your group/team.

SESSION OUTLINES

INTRODUCTORY SESSION (OPTIONAL)

We encourage you to consider holding an introductory session for *Experiencing LeaderShift Together* for these reasons:

1. It gives you an opportunity to distribute the *Experiencing LeaderShift Together* Participant's Guides to ensure that all your members have their own copy before session 1. As you distribute these, let everyone know that this is where they'll follow along with each session's teaching, take notes, and complete applications and assessments.

2. It gives you an opportunity to whet your members' appetites and prime the pump for what this study is all about. You can cast a vision for discovering God's specific calling for their life within the body of Christ.

3. It gives you an opportunity to assess where each person is in his or her current ministry involvement in the body of Christ. What are your members doing? How do they feel about what they're doing? To what degree are they a success at it? How well do they understand the reasons for what they're doing?

You can build this introductory session around the "Introduction" included in the Participant's Guide (and reprinted below). This introduction focuses on four key concepts in a biblical perspective of success. (You'll see this biblical definition of success discussed at length in chapter 3 of *Experiencing LeaderShift*, and you can refer to that chapter for help in explaining these four key concepts.)

Welcome to *Experiencing LeaderShift Together*

Note to leader: **As you welcome your members together, you may want to convey the following in your own words (it's also included in the Introduction and Welcome in the Participant's Guide, page 11).**

Welcome to *Experiencing LeaderShift Together*. This study is the third resource in the *Experiencing LeaderShift* system. Here's a list of all three resources:

1. *Experiencing LeaderShift*—While this book is written primarily for leaders, it's applicable for anyone who wants to participate fully as a member of the body of Christ.

2. The *Experiencing LeaderShift Application Guide* is designed to help leaders do a more effective job of equipping others to function as members of the body of Christ.

3. *Experiencing LeaderShift Together*, which you're beginning now, together with others. Here's a summary of what it's all about:

> *Equipping each of* **you**
> *to play your God-ordained role*
> *in helping* **us** *function*
> *as the body of Christ*

Note to leader: **Emphasize this point: "This is about *you* individually and *us* together."**

Prayer Together

At some point in this session, take a few moments to commit yourself, one another, and this study to the Lord. You may want to ask others to join with you in praying.

Warm-up Questions

The following questions can help get everyone interacting with one another and thinking about their participation in the body of Christ. You may want to divide into smaller groups for this interaction.

1. In what ways have you served in the body of Christ?

2. What one word best describes your experiences with serving in the body of Christ? (And explain why you chose that word.)

3. What one word best captures what you would like your serving experience to be? (And explain.)

How God Defines Success

Note to leader: **This section is also included in the Participant's Guide, page 13.**

As you begin *Experiencing LeaderShift Together,* it is good to focus on a biblical definition of "success" in life and ministry. Given the emphasis our culture places on money, status, awards, titles, and the like, it's easy to lose sight of what God holds up as truly being worthy of recognition.

The primary goal of this study is to help you be a smashing success as God defines it:

—Being Faithful

—Bearing Fruit

—Experiencing Fulfillment

—Making God Famous

Note to leader: **Encourage your members to turn to the Bible passages connected with each concept as you walk through the explanations below, so they can see for themselves how God measures success.**

Being Faithful

In the parable of the talents (Matt. 25:14–30), it's profound to note that the master commended faithfulness: What did you do with what I gave you? The second servant received the exact same commendation as the first servant, even though he produced less of a return. Jesus is making the point that being a faithful steward of what you've been given is what matters most.

Are you being faithful?

Bearing Fruit

In John 15:1–11, Jesus taught that it's God's will that we bear much fruit. As we do so, God is glorified, and we prove to be Christ's disciples.

The New Testament speaks of two kinds of fruit:

1. The fruit of Christlike *character* (Gal. 5:22–23). The fruit of the Holy Spirit includes nine characteristics that should fittingly describe those who call themselves Christians.

2. The fruit of Christlike *influence* (Acts 10:38). We're called to make a difference in the world in the name of Jesus.

Are you bearing fruit?

Experiencing Fulfillment

Looking again at the parable of the talents, the master told his faithful servants, "Enter into the joy of your master" (Matt. 25:21, 23).

Jesus concluded His teaching about fruit-bearing in John 15 with this statement: "These things I have spoken to you [about bearing fruit] so that My joy may be in you, and that your joy may be made full" (John 15:11).

After Jesus sent out seventy disciples on a ministry mission, we read that they "returned with joy" (Luke 10:17). Their personal experience in serving resulted in joy for them.

The result of being faithful and bearing fruit is joy … fulfillment … soul satisfaction.

Are you experiencing fulfillment?

Making God Famous

God wants us to be faithful, to bear fruit, and to experience fulfillment (His joy) in a way that *makes Him famous.* Peter teaches that the faithful exercise of our giftedness is "so that in all things *God may be glorified*" (1 Peter 4:10–11). Jesus tells us, *"My Father is glorified by this,* that you bear much fruit, and so prove to be My disciples" (John 15:8). And He commands us, "Let your light shine before men in such a way that they may see your good works, and *glorify your Father* who is in heaven" (Matt. 5:16).

Are you making God famous?

(*Note:* You can learn much more about how God defines success in chapter 3, "The Success Heresy," in the book *Experiencing LeaderShift.*)

Assessment

Note to leader: **The nine assessment questions listed below are also included in the Participant's Guide, pages 15–16. These can be approached in three different ways:**

> *Option 1:* **Go through the questions one by one, and have each person respond aloud to each one. As the leader, acknowledge each member's answers in a positive and encouraging way.**

> *Option 2:* **Take a few moments for the entire group to write their answers in their**

copy of the Participant's Guide on page 15. You can then discuss these responses together in much the same way as in option 1.

Option 3: (This option requires less time.) Hand each person a sheet of paper, and have them write on it their answers to these questions. Ask them to put their name on the paper, and let them know you'll be collecting the papers. Explain that this will help you understand better how they see themselves and their ministry at this time.

Below are some questions to help you evaluate and pinpoint where you currently are in ministry to others.

(For the first five questions, answer using a scale of 1 to 10—1 = low, 10 = high.)

1. As you think about what God has given you, to what degree do you currently see yourself as being faithful in putting it to use? _____ Explain.

2. To what degree is the fruit of the Spirit evident in who you are as a person? _____ Explain.

3. To what degree are you bearing the fruit of Christlike influence in your world? _____ Explain.

4. To what degree are you experiencing fulfillment in your life and ministry? _____ Explain.

5. To what degree is your life serving to make God famous? _____ Explain.

6. Do you know what your spiritual gifts are? *Check the best answer:*

    __ Not a clue.

    __ I have some idea.

    __ I have a pretty good idea.

    __ Confirmed and affirmed by experience.

7. Have you identified an area of ministry service for which you feel passionate? If so, what is it? _____

8. To what degree are you using your spiritual gift(s) in an area of passion?

    __ I'm not.

    __ I'm using my gift(s) but not with passion.

    __ I'm passionate about my involvement, but I'm not sure I'm using my gift(s).

    __ The phrase "gift-based, passion-driven" is a perfect description for my serving involvement.

9. In ministry to others, do you feel you're serving more *as an individual* or more *as a member of a team?* Pick a number between 1 and 10 to describe your experience: ____
    (1 = I'm an individual servant; 10 = I'm a teammate.)

Looking Ahead

As the leader, make it clear when and where everyone is to meet for session 1. Remind them to bring their copy of the Participant's Guide and their Bible.

You can close this introductory session by praying along these lines: "Father, help each of us to become a smashing success as *You* define success."

SESSION 1

THE ZONE OF GOD'S ANOINTING

For the Leader

This session is tied directly to the content of chapter 9 ("The Zone of God's Anointing") in the book *Experiencing LeaderShift*. You may want to reread that chapter as you prepare for this session—as well as review chapter 3 ("The Success Heresy"), which explains success from a biblical perspective.

Objectives

One of your primary goals as an equipping leader is to help all of your members to identify a serving involvement that will enable them be a "success"—to be *faithful,* to bear *fruit,* and to experience *fulfillment* in a way that makes God *famous.*

For this to happen, they'll need to discover the "zone of God's anointing" for them. This first session is designed to help them accomplish that.

This session has three primary objectives:

1. To help your members fully understand and gain a vision for what it means to serve from the zone of God's anointing—where the Holy Spirit is expressing His presence and power through their lives as they serve others by using their spiritual gifts in a place of ministry passion.

2. To help each member discover or affirm his or her spiritual gifts and God-given passion (the zone of God's anointing).

3. For you as a leader to learn how each member is gifted and impassioned to serve.

Icebreaker (optional; 5–8 minutes)
Refer back to the icebreaker ideas in the "For Leaders Only" section at the front of this Leader's Guide. These can help you transition everyone's thoughts and attention toward this week's session. Be sure not to spend too much time on this.

Prayer Together
Ask the Father to pour out His Holy Spirit upon you as you meet.

Learning Together

Note to leader: **The remaining content in this session is included in the Participant's Guide, starting on page 17—except for text in bold (like this), which is directed toward you as the leader.**

Introduction
Note to leader: **Have someone read this introduction aloud as a way to launch into the focus of this session.**

Everyone likes to be involved in things they're good at. We can all think back to our school years and recall subjects and activities we looked forward to—and others we dreaded. Some of us wished that PE stood for "permanently excused"; others wished it was held twice a day, every day. Some of us were glad when art was no longer required; for others, art class was the highlight of our day. It's probably accurate to say our feelings about those subjects had a lot to do with what we were good at doing.

We can also think back to activities and interests that stirred our passion and devotion, while others stirred little more than daydreams. We brought our whole heart to some things and no heart to others.

We see this in others as well. We all know what it's like to be with people who are passionate about what they're doing, as well as with people who are simply going through the motions.

Why are all of us good at some things and not so good at others? Why does it seem so easy and natural to bring our whole heart to some involvements, while we struggle so much with others?

One of the primary explanations for this is related to God's design of us. In this first session, we'll begin looking at how He's designed us—and the implication of that design for our participation in His work.

God's desire is that we be engaged in doing what we're good at, so we reflect His design. He wants us to find it easy and natural to apply our whole heart to what we do.

Warm-up Questions (10 minutes)

As a group, answer some or all of these questions:

1. Complete this statement: During my school-age years, I came to see that I was good at … (name one or two things) and not so good at …

2. What correlation do you see between what you were good at doing and what you did or didn't enjoy doing? Explain.

3. Can you identify an activity or involvement, past or present, that you bring your whole heart to?

4. Can you identify an activity or involvement, past or present, that you struggle to bring your whole heart to?

DVD Teaching (13 minutes)

Watch the DVD teaching segment for session 1. As you listen, take notes of the points you consider especially helpful or significant.

This teaching segment presents five primary points:

1. Every believer needs to identify his or her spiritual gift(s).

2. Every believer needs to identify a place of ministry passion where his or her gifts can be expressed in serving others.

3. When your spiritual gifts are being expressed in a ministry you're passionate about, you're in the zone of God's anointing.

4. Serving from the zone of His anointing is a key to being successful as God defines success—being faithful, bearing fruit, and experiencing fulfillment, all in a way that makes God famous.

5. As the body of Christ, it's important that we recognize the zone of God's anointing for others.

Key Bible Passage

These words from Paul in 1 Corinthians 12 and 13 serve as a biblical foundation for this session's content.

Note to leader: Be familiar with these passages (pages 19–20 in the Participant's Guide) before you lead this session. As time permits, you may want to lead your group through each one, high-lighting the main truths.

[1] Now concerning spiritual gifts, brethren, I do not want you to be unaware. [2] You know that when you were pagans, you were led astray to the mute idols, however you were led. [3] Therefore I make known to you that no one speaking by the Spirit of God says, "Jesus is accursed"; and no one can say, "Jesus is Lord," except by the Holy Spirit.

[4] Now there are varieties of gifts, but the same Spirit. [5] And there are varieties of ministries, and the same Lord. [6] There are varieties of effects, but the same God who works all things in all persons.

[7] But to each one is given the manifestation of the Spirit for the common good. [8] For to one is given the word of wisdom through the Spirit, and to another the word of knowledge according to the same Spirit; [9] to another faith by the same Spirit, and to another gifts of healing by the one Spirit, [10] and to another the effecting of miracles, and to another prophecy, and to another the distinguishing of spirits, to another various kinds of tongues, and to another the interpretation of tongues. [11] But one and the same Spirit works all these things, distributing to each one individually just as He wills. (1 Cor. 12:1–11)

Notes on this passage for the leader:

Verse 1—**Believers cannot afford to be unaware of spiritual gifts, which play a critical role in the functioning of the body of Christ.**

Verse 4—**There is one Holy Spirit, but a variety of spiritual gifts.**

Verse 5—**There is one Lord, but a variety of ministries.**

Verse 6—**There is a variety of ministry results, but all are accomplished by God through the expression of our spiritual gifts.**

Verse 7—**Every believer has at least one spiritual gift intended to be used for the good of the body.**

Verses 8–10—**Some of the spiritual gifts are listed here.**

Verse 11—**The Holy Spirit distributes our gifts. He decides which specific gifts we possess.**

[1] If I speak with the tongues of men and of angels, but do not have love, I have become a noisy gong or a clanging cymbal. [2] And if I have the gift of prophecy, and know all mysteries and all knowledge; and if I have all faith, so as to remove mountains, but do not have love, I am nothing. [3] And if I give all my possessions to feed the poor, and if I surrender my body to be burned, but do not have love, it profits me nothing.

[4] Love is patient, love is kind and is not jealous; love does not brag and is not arrogant, [5] does not act unbecomingly; it does not seek its own, is not provoked, does not take into account a wrong suffered, [6] does not rejoice in unrighteousness, but rejoices with the truth; [7] bears all things, believes all things, hopes all things, endures all things.

[8] Love never fails; but if there are gifts of prophecy, they will be done away; if there are tongues, they will cease; if there is knowledge, it will be done away. [9] For we know in part, and we prophesy in part; [10] but when the perfect comes, the partial will be done away. [11] When I was a child, I used

to speak like a child, think like a child, reason like a child; when I became a man, I did away with childish things. [12] For now we see in a mirror dimly, but then face to face; now I know in part, but then I shall know fully just as I also have been fully known. [13] But now faith, hope, love, abide these three; but the greatest of these is love. (1 Cor. 13:1–13)

Notes on this passage for the leader: **Love is the glue that holds the body of Christ together. Love is to be the motivation behind all we do in the body of Christ. God *is* love; therefore, to love one another is to imitate God. One of the primary ways we express our love for one another is through serving one another.**

Discussion (20–30 minutes)
Your discussion of these questions is the most important part of this session.

> *Reminders to the leader:*
> - **Ask the Lord to give you wisdom as you lead the discussion in this crucial part of the session.**
> - **For this discussion, it may be helpful to divide into smaller groups of three or four.**
> - **Use as many of the listed questions as time allows.**
>   1. Can you think back upon any serving experiences that represent for you what it means to be in a "zone"? Explain.
>
>   2. Why do you suppose God distributes spiritual gifts to the members of His body? List as many reasons as you can.
>
>   3. How do you explain the fact that each of us is more passionate about certain ministries than we are others?
>
>   4. What do you believe to be your primary spiritual gift(s)? How can you know this is something God has given you?

Note: Later in this session you'll find a "Spiritual Gift Assessment" and a "Ministry Passion Assessment" to complete on your own. We strongly encourage you to complete this assessment, even if you believe you already know your spiritual gifts and passion.

5. Using a scale of 1 to 10, to what degree are you currently using your spiritual gift(s) in serving the body of Christ? ___ (1 = not really using my gifts; 10 = fully using them)

6. What dimension of God's work are you most passionate about being involved in?

7. Using a scale of 1 to 10, to what degree are you using your gift(s) in an area of passion? ___ (1 = not at all; 10 = fully serving in a place of passion)

8. How do you complete this statement?
"God made me _____,
and when I _____,
I feel His pleasure."

9. What would be different about your serving involvement if you were fully serving from the zone of God's anointing?

10. Why do you think it is important for each of us to know how others are gifted and impassioned?

For Ministry Teams

The following questions are designed for ministry teams (people who all serve together in the same specific ministry).

1. Make a list of all the spiritual gifts already present on your ministry team. Take note of how many times each of the gifts appear.

2. Are there any gifts needed on your team that are noticeably missing? Are there any gifts your team needs more of? Name them.

3. What can you do as a team to pursue members who possess these "missing gifts"?

4. What passions do your team members share in common?

5. What other ministry passions are present among your team members?

6. What, if anything, would change in your ministry if all the team members were serving from the zone of God's anointing?

7. What changes would need to be made to have all the members serving from their zone?

Scripture Memory

Commit one or more of these verses to memory. Feel free to use whatever translation you feel most comfortable with. (They're listed here from the *New American Standard Bible*.)

Now concerning spiritual gifts, brethren, I do not want you to be unaware. (1 Cor. 12:1)
But to each one is given the manifestation of the Spirit for the common good. (1 Cor. 12:7)

But one and the same Spirit works all these things, distributing to each one individually just as He wills. (1 Cor. 12:11)

Application Zone

Application / Assessment

The "Ministry Passion Assessment" and the "Spiritual Gift Assessment" below are intended to assist you in discovering or affirming your spiritual gifts and passion. Before the group meets again for the next session, take a few minutes to complete these assessments on your own.

You may already have a clear idea of your gifts and passion. If so, think of these assessments as a way to affirm what you believe to be true, as well as to familiarize yourself with these tools in order to help others.

If you don't clearly know your gifts and passion, these assessments are designed to help point you in the right direction. They aren't intended to be a *definitive* conclusion on your gifts and passion, but rather a starting point for discovery.

Note: For a more comprehensive understanding of your spiritual gifts using four unique assessments, see *Discover Your Spiritual Gifts the Network Way* by Bruce Bugbee. For a more complete understanding of your "Servant Profile"—your spiritual gifts, ministry passion, and personal style—see *What You Do Best in the Body of Christ* (Bruce Bugbee) or *Network* (Bruce Bugbee and Don Cousins) at www.BruceBugbee.com.

Note to leader: Encourage each person to complete these assessments (pages 24–39 in the Participant's Guide) before you meet together for session 2. Let your members know that you'd like them to share the results of these assessments at your next meeting. You should also follow up personally with your members to discuss what they learned from these assessments.

Spiritual Gift Assessment

This assessment is like a mirror of the particular spiritual gifts God has given *you* through His Holy Spirit (1 Cor. 12:7, 11, 18). It's intended to help you identify behaviors you display that correlate with certain spiritual gifts.

As you take this assessment, think about your ministry and life experiences. Your spiritual gift is about what you do best in the body of Christ.

Directions

Following these instructions, you'll find a list of 115 statements. Following that list is an answer grid with 115 boxes, corresponding to each statement in the list.

1. Read each statement, and think about how descriptive it is of *you*. Don't think about what you *should* be or *want* to be, but just who you really are—the person God has gifted you to be.

2. Choose a number from **0 to 3** that reflects how accurately each statement describes you.

    Use this scale:

    3 = definitely and consistently true of me

    2 = usually describes me; true most of the time

    1 = true once in a while; sometimes describes me

    0 = never true of me

3. Record your answer for each statement in the matching numbered box in the answer grid that follows the list of statements. Do this for all 115 statements.

4. After recording all 115 answers, go to the answer grid and add up your numbered answers in each vertical column of boxes. Write in the totals where indicated.

5. Identify your *three highest scores,* and notice the letter listed beneath each one. Transfer those letters to the chart labeled "My Highest Three Scores." Use the key below the chart to determine the three spiritual gifts that most closely match your answers.

Spiritual Gift Assessment Statements

1. When I meet new people, I like them.
2. Because I see God's truth so clearly in a situation, I'm compelled to speak up about it quickly.
3. I act with confidence in God's ability to overcome obstacles.
4. I help people identify the root of their relational and spiritual problems and struggles.
5. I'm handy with tools, making things to serve and support the ministry.
6. I seem to have insight into a person or situation, though I can't explain how I arrived at that knowledge.

7. I find others seeking my advice before they make important decisions.

8. I like to plan and creatively organize people and resources to accomplish ministry goals.

9. I enjoy nurturing people in the context of a long-term relationship where we can grow together.

10. I am strongly motivated to pray over people who are sick, and have seen the healing power of God released in response to my prayers.

11. I confront those who are straying spiritually, helping them remain faithful in their walk with Christ.

12. I have this deep inner compulsion to pray on behalf of others or for some cause or event.

13. I'm highly motivated to see people understand and apply Bible truths in everyday life.

14. People say my prayers have led to unexplainable supernatural signs and wonders.

15. I manage my finances and simplify my lifestyle so I can give as much as possible to the Lord's work.

16. I have the ability to communicate the gospel with clarity and conviction.

17. The Holy Spirit prompts me to speak in a language I don't normally use in order to convey His message.

18. The way I say or do things awakens the truth in others, who then say, "I've never thought of it [or seen or heard it] that way before."

19. I have a tender heart and want to help the hurting, forgotten, and neglected.

20. I can easily see what needs to be done, and I want to do it.

21. Within the context of worship, I hear someone speak in a language that requires an interpretation that I'm able to provide, by the power of the Holy Spirit.

22. I seem to be at my best when identifying goals and motivating others toward their accomplishment.

23. I have a vision for ministry in and through the local church, and an ability to create new ministries to express that vision.

24. I enjoy organizing get-togethers and hosting them.

25. I express God's truth in order to comfort and build up other believers.

26. I have a special ability to trust God for extraordinary needs in challenging circumstances.

27. I recognize the presence of evil and angelic spirits.

28. I find great joy in honoring God with my hand-crafted gifts.

29. I seem to find and understand biblical truths that most people overlook.

30. I readily see the solution to perplexing dilemmas in a person's life or ministry.

31. Once I know the goal, I'll reach it in the most effective and efficient ways possible.

32. My heart breaks to see believers wandering around in need of personal or spiritual direction.

33. I'm compelled to pray for the sick and injured, and have seen many healed.

34. I give the hope of God's promises to those who are discouraged and in need of direction.

35. I'm aware of spiritual battles being waged in individual lives, in the church, and in our culture, and I feel compelled to spend a great deal of time in prayer.

36. I tend to accumulate more biblical content than I'm able to communicate in the time I have.

37. God uses me to demonstrate His miraculous power to overcome the natural order of things.

38. I seem to have a special ability to make money in order to contribute to the cause of Christ.

39. I look for opportunities to talk with unbelievers about spiritual matters.

40. I speak in worship settings with an unknown language that's interpreted by another to build up the church.

41. I notice details like colors, textures, transitions, and moods and how they work together to create meaning.

42. I'm motivated to care for the confused and downcast.

43. I view tasks as a way to support others and help them to better use their gifts.

44. I'm able to give an interpretation to a message spoken in tongues.

45. I'm adept at selecting team members who can work together.

46. I relate well with people from a variety of cultural, geographical, and spiritual backgrounds.

47. I find most people interesting, and I'm able to make them feel welcome in my home.

48. I've exposed sin or deception in others in order to edify and reconcile them.

49. I motivate others with a vision of God that often stretches their faith.

50. I often have a "sixth sense" about what's going on in people, and I'm able to accurately assess their character.

51. I like to design something in my head, then work with tangible materials to create it.

52. I'm able to know certain things as a result of an impression, a vision, or a dream.

53. I'm able to apply spiritual truth in specific and practical ways.

54. I approach ministry logically, making lists of what needs to be done, in what order.

55. I desire to teach, confront, encourage, or correct others in order to prepare them to fulfill their calling.

56. I've been used by God to bring emotional and spiritual healing to others.

57. I like to come alongside those who are weak, wavering, and wondering, to give them help and hope.

58. I'm compelled by the Spirit to pray at times for people or circumstances I don't fully understand.

59. I like to organize biblical truth and present it systematically.

60. After the truths of His Word have been proclaimed, God uses me to manifest His miraculous power.

61. I dream about the good that could be accomplished for God's glory when ministries are adequately funded.

62. I like to come up with new ways to present the gospel.

63. I speak in tongues, with someone else giving an interpretation.

64. Working through one or more art forms, I express my artistic abilities to serve others.

65. I attempt to alleviate or remove the sources of another's suffering.

66. I do whatever is needed when called upon to do so.

67. In a worship gathering, I hear someone speaking in a language unknown to the audience and I am able to interpret so there is understanding.

68. People respond positively to my goals and initiatives.

69. I'm entrepreneurial, adventurous, and willing to take risks to advance the cause of Christ.

70. I'm a warm and accepting person who's able to make others feel welcome and accepted.

71. I'm able to reveal God's perspective and to speak with clarity to a person, church, or culture.

72. I believe the promises of God, and I inspire others to do the same.

73. I'm able to detect heresy, mental illness, or an evil presence.

74. I enjoy working creatively with wood, cloth, paints, metal, glass, and other materials.

75. God gives me insight or revelation that I couldn't have known by any natural means.

76. I seem to have more common sense than most other people.

77. When I see ministries in organizational chaos, I want to develop structures and systems to make them function more effectively.

78. Through trust and care, I build confidence in those I guide and oversee.

79. When I hear of illness, disease, or brokenness in others, my faith leads me to believe God will heal and restore them.

80. People feel safe with me and seem comfortable telling me things they haven't told others.

81. I exercise the spiritual authority God has given us in prayer for His power and protection.

82. I like to be precise and accurate in using the right words when sharing truth.

83. I see tangible evidence that my prayers are making a difference.

84. I experience a great sense of joy when I help meet the tangible needs of others.

85. I have a greater interest in introducing people to Christ than I do in discipling them.

86. I experience a deep peace upon hearing the interpretation of a message I've communicated in a language I don't normally use.

87. As an artistic and creative person, I can identify with perfectionists.

88. I see past someone's problems and faults to their value as a person.

89. I have difficulty saying no when asked to help.

90. The interpretation I have of a message spoken in tongues seems to be understandable, timely, and encouraging.

91. In a group setting, I'm more comfortable leading than not leading.

92. I'm drawn to the idea of coordinating and overseeing a number of ministries or churches to accomplish a greater ministry impact.

93. I look forward to meeting the new people God brings into my life each day.

94. I tend to see spiritual realities as "black and white," while others often see gray.

95. I find it natural to trust God for things that others see as impossible.

96. I find it easy to spot hypocrisy, false teaching, or deception, and I desire to bring God's truth to bear.

97. I'm skilled and resourceful to craft things needed to serve people and ministries.

98. I gain understanding about someone apart from any natural means, and am then able to minister to him or her in a special way.

99. In a situation for which there's no clear and direct biblical instruction, I apply the proper scriptural principles to gain God's wisdom.

100. I feel like the "glue" that holds people and processes together in order to complete ministry goals.

101. Commitment and loyalty in relationships are important qualities to me as I protect and care for others.

102. After the Word has been preached, the Spirit prompts me to pray for someone's healing in response to what has been said.

103. In a positive and gracious way, I challenge those who need to be challenged regarding some specific aspect of their life.

104. I feel the Spirit leading me to pray deeply for things He has revealed to me about others, the ministry, etc.

105. I tend to be so focused on content that I find it a challenge to keep my teaching simple and practical.

106. Others report that visible miracles happened through me, in the name of the Lord.

107. I support the work of ministry with sacrificial gifts.

108. I pray for opportunities to share my faith regularly.

109. I refrain from speaking in tongues because I don't know if an interpreter is present.

110. I like finding new and fresh ways to communicate God's truth.

111. I seek to bring comfort in places like hospitals, halfway houses, prisons, and wherever the poor, handicapped, mentally ill, lonely, shut-ins, or strangers are found.

112. I like doing things that free others to do what they do best.

113. I'm drawn toward worship services where people are free to speak in tongues.

114. I'm comfortable saying, "The buck stops here."

115. I'm culturally sensitive and comfortable relating to various ethnic groups in order to pioneer new ministries among them.

Answer Grid

In the boxes below, record your personal rating for each of the 115 statements listed above. Use a scale of **0 to 3** (0 = not true at all of me; 3 = consistently and definitely true of me).

1	2	3	4	5	6	7	8	9	10	11	12	13	14	15	16	17	18	19	20	21	22	23
24	25	26	27	28	29	30	31	32	33	34	35	36	37	38	39	40	41	42	43	44	45	46
47	48	49	50	51	52	53	54	55	56	57	58	59	60	61	62	63	64	65	66	67	68	69
70	71	72	73	74	75	76	77	78	79	80	81	82	83	84	85	86	87	88	89	90	91	92
93	94	95	96	97	98	99	100	101	102	103	104	105	106	107	108	109	110	111	112	113	114	115
total:																						
A	B	C	D	E	F	G	H	I	J	K	L	M	N	O	P	Q	R	S	T	U	V	W

Scoring: Add your answers in each vertical column of the answer grid, then write these totals in the bottom row of boxes, above the letters.

Record your three highest scores in the following chart.

My Highest Three Scores

Score	Letter	Spiritual gift (refer to key below)

Use the key below to assign the name of the three spiritual gifts that most closely match your answers.

Key

A. hospitality

B. prophecy

C. faith

D. discernment

E. craftsmanship

F. word of knowledge

G. word of wisdom

H. administration

I. shepherding

J. healing

K. encouragement

L. intercession

M. teaching

N. miracles

O. giving

P. evangelism

Q. tongues

R. creative communication

S. mercy

T. helps

U. interpretation

V. leadership

W. apostleship

Ministry Passion Assessment

This assessment can help you identify an area of ministry service that reflects God's heart in you.

While your spiritual gifts reveal *what* you do in the body of Christ, your passion reveals *where*—in what area of ministry service.

Before completing the assessment, ask the Lord to make it clear where He would like to see you involved—where He desires to express His heart through your heart. This is a prayer God will certainly answer, as it's His will that you use your spiritual gifts with passion.

> This is the confidence which we have before Him, that if we ask anything according to His will, He hears us. And if we know that He hears us in whatever we ask, we know that we have the requests which we have asked from Him. (1 John 5:14–15)

Part 1—People Groups

Read over the list of people groups carefully. If you're aware of additional groups in your ministry context, add them to the list as well. Then respond to the questions that follow.

parents

infants

parents of infants

preschoolers

parents of preschoolers

elementary school age

middle schoolers

high schoolers

college age

singles

young marrieds

senior adults

divorced

single parents

widowed

addicts

grieving

hospitalized

incarcerated

leaders

poor

special needs

unemployed

unsaved

women facing unplanned pregnancy

others: _____

_____

_____

_____

_____

_____

For each of your answers to the following questions, identify up to three groups of people.

1. What people do you most enjoy spending time with? Who do you relate to most naturally?

    1)

    2)

    3)

2. What people would you most like to be able to impact for the Lord?

    1)

    2)

    3)

3. Which people do you most readily empathize with? (You have a sensitive understanding of what their situation is like.)

    1)

    2)

    3)

4. What specific groups does God most often bring you in contact with?

    1)

    2)

    3)

5. Can you identify any specific seasons/stations of life in which you had "life experiences" that God could now use to help others?

Conclusions

6. Looking back over your responses to those first five questions, do you see any patterns or themes? Do your responses reveal your passion toward any specific groups of people? If so, who?

1)

2)

3)

Part 2—Evangelism or Discipleship?

Jesus said, "Go therefore and make disciples of all the nations, baptizing them in the name of the Father and the Son and the Holy Spirit, teaching them to observe all that I commanded you; and lo, I am with you always, even to the end of the age" (Matt. 28:19–20).

It's often said that this Great Commission emphasizes two dimensions of ministry. The first is *evangelism*—we engage unbelievers, desiring to see them drawn into a relationship with God. It is our prayer that they choose to follow Jesus.

The second dimension is *discipleship*—we teach them all that Jesus commanded.

While each of us is charged with carrying out this Great Commission, experience indicates that most believers are especially passionate about one or the other of these two dimensions. What about you?

7. Where do you desire to place your greatest time and energy? (Circle one.)
   Evangelism / Discipleship

8. Where do you feel most naturally able to make a difference?
   Evangelism / Discipleship

9. Does your own spiritual journey to, and in, Christ point you toward one of the two dimensions? If so, which one? *Evangelism / Discipleship*

10. If the Holy Spirit were to use you powerfully on one side or the other and gave you the choice, which would you choose? *Evangelism / Discipleship*

11. While most spiritual gifts can be expressed through any passion, you may sense a pull to use your gifts with a particular focus. If so, which of the two dimensions would you choose to focus your gifts toward? *Evangelism / Discipleship*

Conclusions

12. Looking back over your responses to questions 7–11, which dimension of the Great Commission do you seem to have the greatest passion for accomplishing? *Evangelism / Discipleship*

Part 3—Ministry Areas

Read over this list of ministry areas. If you're aware of additional areas of ministry opportunity, feel free to add to this list. Then respond to the questions that follow.

worship arts—drama, media, music, sound, lighting

equipping ministries—leadership development, servant training, gift/passion identification, ministry placement

pastoral care—recovery ministry, counseling, benevolence, prison ministry

evangelism—community service, cross-cultural missions, sports ministry, seeker small groups, apologetics

support ministries—hospitality, event organization, facilities and property management, office assistance, technology services

stewardship ministries—financial counseling

small group ministry

family ministry—men's ministry, women's ministry, youth ministry, children's ministry, single-parent ministry, young married ministry

health care—medical services, nutrition, physical fitness

social concerns—abortion, social injustice, world hunger, the environment, the AIDS crisis

other: _____

_____

_____

_____

For each of your answers in this group of questions, identify up to three ministry areas.

13. Identify the ministry areas that you see being in need of what God has equipped you to offer.

    1)

    2)

    3)

14. In what ministry areas would you most like to participate?

    1)

    2)

    3)

15. A natural talent, life experience, or particular area of expertise may link well with a particular ministry area. Do you see any ministry areas where this may be the case for you?

    1)

    2)

    3)

16. What particular ministry areas has the Holy Spirit put on your heart?

    1)

    2)

    3)

Conclusions

17. Looking back over your responses to the previous four questions, what themes or patterns do you see? What ministry areas appear to be the focus of your passion?

    1)

    2)

    3)

Passion Profile Summary

Copy here your concluding answers from questions 6, 12, and 17.

People groups (question 6):

 a)

 b)

 c)

The Great Commission (circle one): *Evangelism / Discipleship (question 12)*
Ministry categories (question 17):

 a)

 b)

 c)

Conclusion

18. Looking together at your conclusions regarding people groups and ministry areas, do you recognize a particular place or two of ministry service that reflects your passion?

    1)

    2)

19. How could your focus on evangelism or discipleship fit with these ministries?

Now it's time to explore your options. Contact a leader in the area(s) of ministry service you've identified. As you do, continue to pray and ask the Holy Spirit to affirm and confirm where He would like you to use His gifts to you.

Daily Devotions

In the days ahead, the following passages can be read, studied, and reflected upon as a way of reinforcing what has been discussed in this session.

The questions listed below each passage are intended to aid you in your reflection.

Day 1

Read and reflect on Romans 12:1–8.

[1] Therefore I urge you, brethren, by the mercies of God, to present your bodies a living and holy sacrifice, acceptable to God, which is your spiritual service of worship. [2] And do not be conformed to this world, but be transformed by the renewing of your mind, that you may prove what the will of God is, that which is good and acceptable and perfect.

[3] For through the grace given to me I say to everyone among you not to think more highly of himself than he ought to think; but to think so as to have sound judgment, as God has allotted to each a measure of faith. [4] For just as we have many members in one body and all the members do not have the same function, [5] so we, who are many, are one body in Christ, and individually members one of another. [6] Since we have gifts that differ according to the grace given to us, each of us is to exercise them accordingly: if prophecy, according to the proportion of his faith; [7] if service, in his serving; or he who teaches, in his teaching; [8] or he who exhorts, in his exhortation; he who gives, with liberality; he who leads, with diligence; he who shows mercy, with cheerfulness. (Rom. 12:1–8)

1. What does Paul mean by "to present your bodies a living and holy sacrifice, acceptable to God" (v. 1)?

2. How is the presenting of our bodies in that way a "spiritual service of worship" (v. 1)?

3. In what ways are you most tempted to be "conformed to this world" (v. 2)?

4. Where do you need transformation in order to fulfill the will of God (v. 2)?

5. In what ways are you tempted to think more highly of yourself than you should (v. 3)?

6. Think about your "measure of faith" (v. 3). Identify three areas of faith for you—three ways in which you're clearly aware of your dependence on God.

7. What role does "the grace given to us" play in the use of your gifts (v. 6)?

8. What role does faith play in the use of your gifts (v. 6)?

9. Make a list of the spiritual gifts mentioned in verses 6–8.

Day 2

Read and reflect on 1 Peter 4:8–11.

[8] Above all, keep fervent in your love for one another, because love covers a multitude of sins. [9] Be hospitable to one another without complaint. [10] As each one has received a special gift, employ it in serving one another as good stewards of the manifold grace of God. [11] Whoever speaks, is to do so as one who is speaking the utterances of God; whoever serves is to do so as one who is serving by the strength which God supplies; so that in all things God may be glorified through Jesus Christ, to whom belongs the glory and dominion forever and ever. Amen. (1 Peter 4:8–11)

1. What does it mean for us to remain "fervent" in our love for one another, and why is this so important (v. 8)?

2. In what ways is that "love covers a multitude of sins" (v. 8)?

3. In what specific and practical ways can we "be hospitable to one another" (v. 9)?

4. Why do you suppose Peter adds the phrase "without complaint" at the end of verse 9?

5. *Who* are we to serve with our gifts, according to verse 10?

6. What does it mean to be "stewards of the manifold grace of God" (v. 10)? How do we steward His grace?

7. In what ways can God be glorified (v. 11) through the use of our gifts as we serve one another?

_____

Day 3

Read and reflect on John 15:1–11.

¹ I am the true vine, and My Father is the vinedresser. ² Every branch in Me that does not bear fruit, He takes away; and every branch that bears fruit, He prunes it so that it may bear more fruit. ³ You are already clean because of the word which I have spoken to you. ⁴ Abide in Me, and I in you. As the branch cannot bear fruit of itself unless it abides in the vine, so neither can you unless you abide in Me. ⁵ I am the vine, you are the branches; he who abides in Me and I in him, he bears much fruit, for apart from Me you can do nothing. ⁶ If anyone does not abide in Me, he is thrown away as a branch and dries up; and they gather them, and cast them into the fire and they are burned. ⁷ If you abide in Me, and My words abide in you, ask whatever you wish, and it will be done for you.

[8] My Father is glorified by this, that you bear much fruit, and so prove to be My disciples. [9] Just as the Father has loved Me, I have also loved you; abide in My love. [10] If you keep My commandments, you will abide in My love; just as I have kept My Father's commandments and abide in His love. [11] These things I have spoken to you so that My joy may be in you, and that your joy may be made full. (John 15:1–11)

1. What is Jesus referring to when He speaks of bearing fruit in verse 2?

2. How does God prune us so that we "bear more fruit" (v. 2)?

3. What does it mean to "abide" in Jesus (v. 4)?

4. How does our ability to bear fruit depend upon our abiding in Jesus (v. 5)?

5. In what ways does our abiding in Jesus impact our prayer life (v. 7)?

6. How is God glorified when we bear fruit (v. 8)?

7. Why is it important to obey God's commands (v. 10)? List as many reasons as you can.

8. How does our obedience affect our ability to abide (v. 10)?

9. How is our joy affected by our application of the truth in this passage, according to verse 11?

10. How would you explain this joy to someone who doesn't understand it? How does this joy manifest itself in your life (v. 11)?

———

Day 4

Read and reflect on Matthew 25:14–19.

[14] For it is just like a man about to go on a journey, who called his own slaves and entrusted his possessions to them. [15] To one he gave five talents, to another, two, and to another, one, each according to his own ability; and he went on his journey. [16] Immediately the one who had received the five talents went and traded with them, and gained five more talents. [17] In the same manner the one who had received the two talents gained two more. [18] But he who received the one talent went away, and dug a hole in the ground and hid his master's money.

[19] Now after a long time the master of those slaves came and settled accounts with them. (Matt. 25:14–19)

1. Jesus wants His followers to understand something, which prompted His telling of this parable. What do you think it is?

2. Why didn't each slave receive the same number of talents (v. 15)?

3. What implications does verse 15 have for your life?

4. When the first two slaves went out immediately and attempted to invest what they'd been given, what risks were they taking (vv. 16–17)?

5. Why was the third slave unwilling to risk what he'd been given (v. 18)?

6. Why did the master do what he did in verse 19? And what implication does that have for you?

_____

Day 5

Continuing the parable from yesterday, read and reflect on Matthew 25:19–30.

[19] Now after a long time the master of those slaves came and settled accounts with them. [20] The one who had received the five talents came up and brought five more talents, saying, "Master, you entrusted five talents to me. See, I have gained five more talents." [21] His master said to him, "Well done, good and faithful slave. You were faithful with a few things, I will put you in charge of many things; enter into the joy of your master."

[22] Also the one who had received the two talents came up and said, "Master, you entrusted two talents to me. See, I have gained two more talents." [23] His master said to him, "Well done, good and faithful slave. You were faithful with a few things, I will put you in charge of many things; enter into the joy of your master."

[24] And the one also who had received the one talent came up and said, "Master, I knew you to be a hard man, reaping where you did not sow and gathering where you scattered no seed. [25] And I was afraid, and went away and hid your talent in the ground. See, you have what is yours."

[26] But his master answered and said to him, "You wicked, lazy slave, you knew that I reap where I did not sow and gather where I scattered no seed. [27] Then you ought to have put my money in the bank, and on my arrival I would have received my money back with interest. [28] Therefore take away the talent from him, and give it to the one who has the ten talents. [29] For to everyone

who has, more shall be given, and he will have an abundance; but from the one who does not have, even what he does have shall be taken away. [30] Throw out the worthless slave into the outer darkness; in that place there will be weeping and gnashing of teeth." (Matt. 25:19–30)

1. In verses 21 and 23, the master commends the first two slaves. What did these slaves receive as a result of being faithful?

2. What do verses 21 and 23 have in common? Why is this significant?

3. In your own words, what explanation did the last slave give for his actions (vv. 24–25)?

4. Why didn't the master find his explanation acceptable (vv. 26–27)?

5. For this third slave, what were the consequences of not being faithful (vv. 28–30)?

6. What can you learn from this parable? List as many insights as you can.

SESSION 2

GOD'S PLAN FOR HIS CHURCH

For the Leader

This session is tied directly to the content of chapter 6 ("The Organizational Heresy") in *Experiencing LeaderShift*. You may want to reread that chapter in preparation for this session. In addition, reviewing the content in chapter 4 ("The Serving Heresy") and chapter 8 ("The Blessing Factor") will help you understand more fully why God has called each member of the body of Christ to participate in the work of His kingdom.

Objectives

In session 1, we focused on answering this question: "How has God equipped *me* to participate in the work of His kingdom?"

Now in session 2 we move to this question: "How has God equipped *us* to participate *together* in the work of His kingdom?" As Paul explains in 1 Corinthians 12, we are all individual members of a *body,* functioning in relationship to each other.

Here are the four primary objectives for this session:

1. For all of your members to share what they believe to be their spiritual gifts and passion (their "zone")—so that everyone is (a) aware of how each member is equipped to serve and (b) able to affirm one another's gifts and passion.

2. For each person to clearly understand that he or she is not to serve alone or in isolation but rather as a member of the body of Christ.

3. For each person to begin discovering how his or her role and contribution will complement the roles and contributions of others in the body.

4. To begin seeing more clearly God's plan for His church as revealed in Ephesians 4:11–16.

Icebreaker (optional; 5–8 minutes)

Again, refer back to the icebreaker ideas in the "For Leaders Only" section at the front of this Leader's Guide.

Some particularly good icebreaker questions to ask for this session could be

What is one of your clearest and fondest memories of God working through your life to make a difference?

Complete this statement: I would like to have more opportunities to make a difference by.…

Prayer Together

You may want to focus especially on thanking God for His gift to us of the church. Express your gratitude specifically for the many blessings and benefits we receive through the church.

Learning Together

Note to leader: **The remaining content in this session is included in the Participant's Guide, starting on page 49—except for text in bold (like this), which is directed toward you as the leader.**

Introduction

Note to leader: **Have someone read this aloud.**

Today's culture focuses on the individual. Individualism is pushed so heavily that each of us is taught from an early age to learn to stand on our own. The very notion of depending on others is frowned upon and seen as a sign of weakness.

How strange, then, that God tells us in His Word that He has made us to depend upon one another—and even to need each other. Our culture's emphasis on individualism meets complete and total contradiction from the teaching of the Bible.

Perhaps nowhere is this truth stated more clearly in the Bible than in 1 Corinthians 12. Here Paul draws the analogy between the church and the human body. The picture of the human body serves as the perfect example of individual parts (members) working in concert with other individual parts. It's an easy analogy to understand: one body, many parts. This explains why we're called "members of the body of Christ." While each of us has our own role, we're to function in that role as members of the body for the common good.

As Paul explains, this means that some have a big role, others a smaller one. Some have a visible role; others participate behind the scenes. Whatever the case, Paul makes it clear that we're all individual members of the same body, and each person's contribution is vital to the body working as God intended.

In this session, we'll begin looking at God's design for us as the body of Christ. We'll take time to learn about one another as individuals; then we'll move to discovering how we're to partner with each other in functioning as Christ's body.

Warm-up Questions (10 minutes)

Answering these questions can help everyone understand and "feel" the truth of "many members—one body."

1. What part of your body do you think you could most easily do without?

2. How would this lost part affect your body as a whole?

3. What impact would this lost part have on the quality of your life as a whole?

4. If you had to lose one of your five senses, which would you choose to lose first?

5. What effect would that "missing sense" have on your body as a whole?

6. Can you think of a very small part of your body that causes the whole body to suffer when it's hurting?

DVD Teaching (14 minutes)

Watch the DVD teaching segment for session 2. As you listen, take notes of the points you consider especially helpful or significant.

This teaching segment presents these four primary points:

1. There are many separate and individual parts, but one body.

2. It's very important to understand how our part fits with all the other parts of the body.

3. We learn from Ephesians 4:11–12 that some members of the body are gifted to *equip,* while other members are gifted to *serve.* (In the next couple of sessions we'll continue to explore the difference between *equippers* and *servers.*)

4. When every individual functions as a member of the body, everyone benefits. These benefits are spelled out in Ephesians 4:13–16.

Key Bible Passage

This session's key Bible passage is Ephesians 4:11–16 (especially vv. 13–16). It helps us understand the benefits of functioning according to God's plan.

[11] And He gave some as apostles, and some as prophets, and some as evangelists, and some as pastors and teachers, [12] for the equipping of the saints for the work of service, to the building up of the body of Christ; [13] until we all attain to the unity of the faith, and of the knowledge of the Son of God, to a mature man, to the measure of the stature which belongs to the fullness of Christ. [14] As a result, we are no longer to be children, tossed here and there by waves and carried about by every wind of doctrine, by the trickery of men, by craftiness in deceitful scheming; [15] but speaking the truth in love, we are to grow up in all aspects into Him who is the head, even Christ, [16] from whom the whole body, being fitted and held together by what every joint supplies, according to the proper working of each individual part, causes the growth of the body for the building up of itself in love. (Eph. 4:11–16)

Notes on this passage for the leader:

Verse 1—Some have been given spiritual gifts that call them to an equipping role in the body of Christ. As such, they become leaders.

Verse 12—Some have been given spiritual gifts that call them to a serving role. These members use their gifts to meet needs in the lives of other members and the body as a whole.

The results of functioning according to the plan laid out in verses 11–12 are spelled out in verses 13–16:

Verse 13—There's a spirit of unity in the body: Members of Christ's body grow in knowing God and in their likeness to Jesus.

Verse 14—They develop truth-filled convictions enabling them to stand firm in a world filled with lies.

Verse 15—They speak the truth to one another in love, and thereby help one another mature.

Verse 16—They complement each other in their respective roles so that all of the members of the body end up receiving what they need. A bond of love holds the body together.

Discussion (20–30 minutes)

Your discussion of these questions is the most important part of this session.

Note to leader: You may choose to divide into smaller groups for this discussion. If you do, plan to revisit questions 3 and 4 in the full group setting once everyone is back together.

1. What is lost or sacrificed when members serve alone instead of together with others?

2. What specifically is gained when we serve in partnership with one another?

3. Describe what you believe to be the zone of God's anointing for you—where your spiritual gift(s) and passion are fully applied. (If you aren't sure, that's okay. This study, plus your ongoing participation in service and continued prayer, will eventually reveal your zone.)

4. As you serve in the body of Christ, can you identify tangible ways in which your contribution is supported and aided by the contribution of others?

5. Can you identify how the gifts of others have been a source of blessing for you as you serve?

6. What will you do differently in your service as a result of this session?

For Ministry Teams

1. To what degree do we serve as separate individuals instead of serving together as members of a unified team? (**Have all the members give their answer to this, based on their own experience.** Use a scale of 1 to 10: 1 = we function only as individual parts; 10 = we truly function as a team, with all individual parts working together as one.)

2. Each person should explain how he or she depends on other team members to make their own contribution. (Be as specific as you can.)

3. To what degree are the members of our team serving from the zone of God's anointing? (Use a scale of 1 to 10: 1 = we serve wherever needed, based on willingness and availability; 10 = our serving can be described as fully gift-based and passion-driven.)

4. In what ways could we increase our unity and effectiveness in serving together?

Application Zone

Application / Assessment

Note to leader: Make sure each member fully understands this assessment (pages 54–57 in the Participant's Guide). Read aloud the explanation provided; then answer any questions that anyone may have.

As the assigned application for this session, we'll be taking the "Anointed Moments Assessment." What is an "anointed moment"? It's a time when the power of God flowed through your life, enabling you to serve someone else. Later, as you reflect back on such moments, you find yourself realizing that "God showed up" while you were involved in that particular activity or involvement; it caused you to think, "I was born to do this."

In these anointed moments, it doesn't matter whether what you did blessed one person or a thousand. What matters is that as you did it, God's power flowed through your life in service to another.

Reserve an hour or two in a quiet place where you can be alone before God and ask Him this question: "In what life and ministry experiences over recent months have You displayed Your power through my life to serve another person?"

Ask God to bring to mind these "anointed moments." Seek to identify ten to twelve of them. For each one, write down a description of what you did, how you felt, and how God used you. What resulted from this service?

Here are a couple of examples:

Example 1: God dispensed His wisdom through me to help a friend make a very difficult decision. A friend called, wanting to discuss a decision she was facing. She admitted she was very confused and wanted to know if I could possibly help. I listened, asked a lot of questions, and then counseled her with what I believed reflected God's wisdom. After listening to what I had to say, this friend affirmed that it made sense to do as I suggested. She did, and the result proved that the counsel I gave was wise. God used me to help guide a friend at a very critical time. It was very fulfilling for me to be used of God to help this friend. She was blessed by what resulted and I was blessed to play a part.

Example 2: The facility that our ministry utilizes was in need of updating. Heavy use over the years had taken a toll. With funds in short supply, ministry leaders didn't want to spend money on the facility. God prompted me to step forward to help. I approached some individuals associated with the ministry who owned businesses that could be of help. They were willing to donate materials at cost. I then approached some skilled workers who were willing to donate their time to help out. I also contacted some volunteers who were willing to pitch in. In the end, the facility received a needed facelift at a minimal cost. While the work was being done, I had the opportunity to encourage those who were helping out. It seemed that everyone had a great experience and enjoyed making a contribution. God gave me ideas and people to contact. He seemingly prepared them for my request for help. I enjoyed bringing everything together and seeing the goal accomplished.

With those examples in mind, record your own list of "anointed moments" in the space below (or if you need more room, use your own paper to write them down).

Note to leader: If possible, schedule a separate meeting with each member to discuss the results of the "Anointed Moments Assessment." This could be done one-on-one (which is most beneficial) or together as a group.

As everyone shares their "anointed moments," listen carefully for the following:

1. **Is it clear that their spiritual gifts are being expressed in these moments? (If they've accurately identified their gifts, they'll be evident in these anointed moments.)**
2. **Do you hear their God-given passion coming through? (Passion and anointing should go hand-in-hand.)**

3. Are certain "patterns" emerging as they share these moments? (For example, was
    the setting for these moments typically with one or two individuals or with larger
    groups? Did these moments involve solving problems or bringing change? Did they
    clearly involve a leadership influence, or more of a support role? Was the situation
    task-oriented or people-oriented?) You'll probably see some patterns emerging.

In the end, here's the key question to answer: *How can this person shape his or her future
serving involvement so that the number of anointed moments is increased?* The ultimate goal is to
structure one's entire life so that it's filled with anointed moments.

My Anointed Moments

1. _____

   _____

   _____

   _____

   _____

2. _____

   _____

   _____

   _____

   _____

3. _____

   _____

   _____

   _____

   _____

4. _____

5. _____

6. _____

7. _____

8. _____

9.

10.

11.

12.

Scripture Memory

Select one or all of the following passages to memorize.

You know of Jesus of Nazareth, how God anointed Him with the Holy Spirit and with power, and how He went about doing good and healing all who were oppressed by the devil, for God was with Him. (Acts 10:38)

We proclaim Him, admonishing every man and teaching every man with all wisdom, so that we may present every man complete in Christ. For this purpose also I labor, striving according to His power, which mightily works within me. (Col. 1:28–29)

Then he said to me, "This is the word of the LORD to Zerubbabel saying, 'Not by might nor by power, but by My Spirit,' says the LORD of hosts." (Zech. 4:6)

And He gave some as apostles, and some as prophets, and some as evangelists, and some as pastors and teachers, for the equipping of the saints for the work of service, to the building up of the body of Christ; until we all attain to the unity of the faith, and of the knowledge of the Son of God, to a mature man, to the measure of the stature which belongs to the fullness of Christ. As a result, we are no longer to be children, tossed here and there by waves and carried about by every wind of doctrine, by the trickery of men, by craftiness in deceitful scheming; but speaking the truth in love, we are to grow up in all aspects into Him who is the head, even Christ, from whom the whole body, being fitted and held together by what every joint supplies, according to the proper working of each individual part, causes the growth of the body for the building up of itself in love. (Eph. 4:11–16)

Daily Devotions

Day 1

Read and reflect on Romans 12:9–21.

[9] Let love be without hypocrisy. Abhor what is evil; cling to what is good. [10] Be devoted to one another in brotherly love; give preference to one another in honor; [11] not lagging behind in diligence, fervent in spirit, serving the Lord; [12] rejoicing in hope, persevering in tribulation, devoted to prayer, [13] contributing to the needs of the saints, practicing hospitality.

[14] Bless those who persecute you; bless and do not curse. [15] Rejoice with those who rejoice, and weep with those who weep. [16] Be of the same mind toward one another; do not be haughty in mind, but associate with the lowly. Do not be wise in your own estimation. [17] Never pay back evil for evil to anyone. Respect what is right in the sight of all men. [18] If possible, so far as it depends on you, be at peace with all men. [19] Never take your own revenge, beloved, but leave room for the wrath of God, for it is written, "Vengeance is Mine, I will repay," says the Lord. [20] "But if your enemy is hungry, feed him, and if he is thirsty, give him a drink; for in so doing you will heap burning coals on his head." [21] Do not be overcome by evil, but overcome evil with good. (Rom. 12:9–21)

1. What does Paul mean by the phrase, "Let love be without hypocrisy" (v. 9)? How does that relate to our need to "abhor what is evil" and "cling to what is good"?

2. Identify three specific ways in which you could apply the command of verse 10.

3. Rewrite verses 11–16 in your own words.

4. Identify three practical applications of these verses (11–16) for your participation in the body of Christ.

5. In what ways is evil often paid back with evil (v. 17)?

6. Paul prefaces the command to "be at peace with all men" (v. 18) by first saying, "If possible, so far as it depends on you...." Why is that preface so important? Why is it so difficult to heed this instruction to be at peace with everyone?

7. Explain what you should do and not do in obedience to verse 19. On a practical level, what does this mean?

8. Have you ever personally applied the command of verses 20–21? What did you do, and what was the result? Why is this so difficult to carry out? Is there a person in your life now to whom you should apply this command?

Day 2

Read and reflect on 1 Corinthians 12:18–31.

[18] But now God has placed the members, each one of them, in the body, just as He desired. [19] If they were all one member, where would the body be? [20] But now there are many members, but one body. [21] And the eye cannot say to the hand, "I have no need of you"; or again the head to the feet, "I have no need of you." [22] On the contrary, it is much truer that the members of the body which seem to be weaker are necessary; [23] and those members of the body which we deem less honorable, on these we bestow more abundant honor, and our less presentable members become much more presentable, [24] whereas our more presentable members have no need of it. But God has so composed the body, giving more abundant honor to that member which lacked, [25] so that there may be no division in the body, but that the members may have the same care for one another. [26] And if one member suffers, all the members suffer with it; if one member is honored, all the members rejoice with it.

[27] Now you are Christ's body, and individually members of it. [28] And God has appointed in the church, first apostles, second prophets, third teachers, then miracles, then gifts of healings, helps,

administrations, various kinds of tongues. [29] All are not apostles, are they? All are not prophets, are they? All are not teachers, are they? All are not workers of miracles, are they? [30] All do not have gifts of healings, do they? All do not speak with tongues, do they? All do not interpret, do they? [31] But earnestly desire the greater gifts. And I show you a still more excellent way. (1 Cor. 12:18–31)

1. How would you explain to someone the truth of verse 18? What are the implications of this truth for your participation in the body of Christ?

2. Why is it so important that there be *many* individual members, yet only *one* body?

3. Identify some examples of "weaker" (v. 22) and "less honorable" (v. 23) members of the body. Why are these members so needed in the body of Christ?

4. In what ways can "division" (v. 25) arise in the body of Christ?

5. What does verse 26 have in common with Romans 12:15 (in yesterday's passage)? In what way could you apply these verses in your current situation?

6. Notice that the list in verse 28 is an ordered one. How do you explain the order given?

7. What are the "greater gifts" referred to in verse 31? Why are we told to "earnestly desire" these gifts?

Day 3

Read and reflect on Ephesians 4:1–7.

[1] Therefore I, the prisoner of the Lord, implore you to walk in a manner worthy of the calling with which you have been called, [2] with all humility and gentleness, with patience, showing tolerance for one another in love, [3] being diligent to preserve the unity of the Spirit in the bond of peace. [4] There is one body and one Spirit, just as also you were called in one hope of your calling; [5] one Lord, one faith, one baptism, [6] one God and Father of all who is over all and through all and in all. [7] But to each one of us grace was given according to the measure of Christ's gift. (Eph. 4:1–7)

1. What does it mean to walk "worthy of the calling" we've received (v. 1)? What is that calling?

2. What's the opposite of the instruction of verse 2? In what ways could you apply verse 2 in your current involvement in the body of Christ?

3. For what reasons is unity so important in the body of Christ? What does it mean to be "diligent to preserve the unity" (v. 3)?

4. On what basis is unity built (vv. 4–6)?

5. What do you believe to be the primary threats to unity in the body of Christ?

6. In what ways is every believer a recipient of grace (v. 7)?

7. Identify three practical action steps you could take to increase the unity of the body of believers you're currently involved in.

Day 4

Read and reflect on Acts 2:42–47.

[42] They were continually devoting themselves to the apostles' teaching and to fellowship, to the breaking of bread and to prayer. [43] Everyone kept feeling a sense of awe; and many wonders and signs were taking place through the apostles. [44] And all those who believed were together and had all things in common; [45] and they began selling their property and possessions, and were sharing them with all, as anyone might have need. [46] Day by day continuing with one mind in the temple, and breaking bread from house to house, they were taking their meals together with gladness and sincerity of heart, [47] praising God and having favor with all the people. And the Lord was adding to their number day by day those who were being saved. (Acts 2:42–47)

1. We're told in verse 42 that these new believers committed themselves to four involvements. How would you describe those four, in your own words?

2. What do you think it means that they "were continually devoting themselves" (v. 42) to these involvements?

3. What would it look like for *you* to be continually devoted to these involvements?

4. Make a list of what resulted from these involvements, according to verses 43–47.

5. What would we see happening today if these same results were to occur?

6. In what ways does your current involvement in the body of Christ line up with Acts 2:42–47?

7. In what ways does your current involvement in the body of Christ *not* line up with verses 42–47?

8. What could you do or change to increase the similarity between what you read in these verses and your current involvement?

Day 5

Read and reflect on 1 Peter 2:1–12.

[1] Therefore, putting aside all malice and all deceit and hypocrisy and envy and all slander, [2] like new-born babies, long for the pure milk of the word, so that by it you may grow in respect to salvation, [3] if you have tasted the kindness of the Lord.

[4] And coming to Him as to a living stone which has been rejected by men, but is choice and precious in the sight of God, [5] you also, as living stones, are being built up as a spiritual house for a holy priesthood, to offer up spiritual sacrifices acceptable to God through Jesus Christ. [6] For this is contained in Scripture: "Behold, I lay in Zion a choice stone, a precious corner stone, and he who believes in Him will not be disappointed." [7] This precious value, then, is for you who believe; but for those who disbelieve, "The stone which the builders rejected, this became the very corner stone," [8] and "A stone of stumbling and a rock of offense"; for they stumble because they are disobedient to the word, and to this doom they were also appointed.

[9] But you are a chosen race, a royal priesthood, a holy nation, a people for God's own possession, so that you may proclaim the excellencies of Him who has called you out of darkness into His marvelous light; [10] for you once were not a people, but now you are the people of God; you had not received mercy, but now you have received mercy.

[11] Beloved, I urge you as aliens and strangers to abstain from fleshly lusts which wage war against the soul. [12] Keep your behavior excellent among the Gentiles, so that in the thing in which they slander you as evildoers, they may because of your good deeds, as they observe them, glorify God in the day of visitation. (1 Peter 2:1–12)

1. What are we to put aside according to verse 1? State this in your own words.

2. What does it mean to "long for the pure milk of the word" (v. 2)?

3. In what practical ways does the Word of God help us "grow in respect to salvation" (v. 2)? (See also 2 Tim. 3:16.)

4. What does the analogy Peter uses in verses 4–5 have in common with Paul's analogy of the body in 1 Corinthians 12?

5. As "the people of God" (v. 10), what is our purpose, as stated in verse 9?

6. What does Peter mean by saying, "for you once were not a people" (v. 10)?

7. What "fleshly lusts" (v. 11) wage war against your soul? What does it mean for you to "abstain" from these fleshly lusts?

8. Why is it so important that we model Christlike behavior (v. 12)?

9. What are the most visible ways you currently live up to verse 12?

SESSION 3

THE EQUIPPER

For the Leader

This session is tied directly to the content of chapter 1 ("Leadership Heresies") in *Experiencing LeaderShift*. You may want to reread that chapter in preparing for this session. Reviewing chapter 6 ("The Organizational Heresy") and chapter 10 ("Transforming Consumers into Contributors") would also be helpful.

Objectives

In our first two sessions we gained a clearer recognition of God's plan for His church. At the heart of this plan is the active participation of every individual believer. God has made it unmistakably clear that the work of His kingdom is not to be left to a select few, but rather should be carried out by all who call Jesus their Lord and Savior. We've also seen that the Holy Spirit distributes gifts to every member of the body, then calls each member to make a contribution based on his or her giftedness.

In this third session, we want to look at a specific calling shared by certain members of the body—the calling to *equip* others for the work of service. We call these people *equippers*.

As we focus on equipping, here are the three primary objectives for this session:

1. To begin making a clear distinction between those who are gifted to equip (equippers) and those who are gifted to serve (servers).

2. To help those with equipping gifts (equippers) gain a clearer vision for their role in the body of Christ.

3. To help those with serving gifts (servers) to better understand the role and contribution of equippers. With this understanding, servers can more clearly grasp the nature of their relationship with equippers.

Icebreaker (optional; 5–8 minutes)

Again, refer to the icebreaker suggestions in the "For Leaders Only" section at the front of this Leader's Guide.

Prayer Together

As an opening prayer, ask God to make His will known to each of you regarding His calling and ministry involvement.

> This is the confidence which we have before Him, that, if we ask anything according to His will, He hears us. And if we know that He hears us in whatever we ask, we know that we have the requests which we have asked from Him. (1 John 5:14–15)

At the end of this session, depending on where your group member are in their understanding of their spiritual gifts and calling, you may want to spend a few minutes asking the Lord to help each person discern the role God has gifted him or her to fill. Or pray over the equippers among you and ask God to anoint their efforts.

Learning Together

Note to leader: **This content is included in the Participant's Guide starting on page 69—except for text in bold (like this), which is for you as the leader.**

Introduction

Note to leader: **Have someone read this aloud.**

In this session, we'll look at the role and contribution of those who have been given gifts of an equipping nature.

In Ephesians 4:11, Paul writes, "And He gave some as apostles, and some as prophets, and some as evangelists, and some as pastors, and teachers." We call these the *equipping gifts,* and we speak of those who possess them as *equippers.* That's because of Paul's next words: "for the *equipping* of the saints for the work of service" (v. 12). The Holy Spirit gives these equipping gifts to "some" members of the body for the express purpose of equipping the *other* members of the body for "the work of service."

This equipping concept is one we should be able to understand from other arenas of life. Parents spend years equipping their children to live on their own. Teachers and professors equip their students with the knowledge they'll need to succeed in an academic or professional field. In the athletic arena, coaches equip their athletes to succeed on the playing field. In the marketplace, employers equip employees to make a valued contribution to the work of the company.

This is exactly what God had in mind when He gave some in His body gifts of apostleship, prophecy, evangelism, pastoring, and teaching. Equippers are to use these gifts to make a contribution in the lives of those who follow them, so that these followers can make a contribution of their own, based on their gifting.

Warm-up Questions (10 minutes)

Answering these questions can help everyone better understand the concept of *equipping.*

1. Identify two or three specific ways in which your parents equipped you to live independently of them.

2. From the arenas of education or extracurricular involvement, can you identify a teacher, coach, or leader who had an equipping role in your life? What exactly did this person do for you, and how did that serve you?

3. Is there someone who currently has an equipping role in your life? If so, explain how this is helping you.

Note to leader: **You may want to allow time at this point for each member to share his or her "anointed moments." This sharing could serve as a session of its own.**

DVD Teaching (12–15 minutes)

Watch the DVD teaching segment for session 3. Once again, take notes on anything you consider particularly helpful or significant.

This teaching segment presents these four primary points:

1. Ephesians 4:11 tells us that "some" in the body of Christ are given spiritual gifts of an equipping nature. They're called to serve as equippers in the body. That word *some* obviously means that not all are gifted or called to a primary role of equipping.

2. The equipping gifts listed in Ephesians 4:11 have some common characteristics:
   — They're people-focused, not task-focused. Without other people listening and following, these gifts cannot be used.
   — When these gifts are used as God intended, other members of the body are equipped to carry out works of service.
   — All of these gifts provide leadership in their own way to the body of Christ.

3. Those who fill positions of leadership must function as equippers if they're to use their gifts as God intended.

4. Equippers have three primary tasks:
   — To help others discover their role in the body (their zone of God's anointing).
   — To create or provide opportunities for others to fulfill their role in the body.
   — To give others the tools they need (the equipping) to make their contribution to the work of God's kingdom.

Key Bible Passage

While Ephesians 4:11–12 is the primary passage for this session, additional verses listed here also speak of the equipping concept. (They're also included in the daily devotionals at the end of this session.)

***Note to leader:* In this first brief passage, note how we see four generations of Christ followers: Paul, Timothy, "faithful men," and "others."**

The things which you have heard from me in the presence of many witnesses, entrust these to faithful men who will be able to teach others also. (2 Tim. 2:2)

After these things the Lord appointed seventy others also, and sent them two by two before His face into every city and place where He Himself was about to go. Then He said to them, "The harvest truly is great, but the laborers are few; therefore pray the Lord of the harvest to send out laborers into His harvest. Go your way; behold, I send you out as lambs among wolves. Carry neither money bag, knapsack, nor sandals; and greet no one along the road. But whatever house you enter, first say, 'Peace to this house.' And if a son of peace is there, your peace will rest on it; if not, it will return to you. And remain in the same house, eating and drinking such things as they give, for the laborer is worthy of his wages. Do not go from house to house. Whatever city you enter, and they receive you, eat such things as are set before you. And heal the sick there, and say to them, 'The kingdom of God has come near to you.' But whatever city you enter, and they do not receive you, go out into its streets and say, 'The very dust of your city which clings to us we wipe off against you. Nevertheless know this, that the kingdom of God has come near you.' But I say to you that it will be more tolerable in that Day for Sodom than for that city.

"Woe to you, Chorazin! Woe to you, Bethsaida! For if the mighty works which were done in you had been done in Tyre and Sidon, they would have repented long ago, sitting in sackcloth and ashes. But it will be more tolerable for Tyre and Sidon at the judgment than for you. And you, Capernaum, who are exalted to heaven, will be brought down to Hades. He who hears you hears Me, he who rejects you rejects Me, and he who rejects Me rejects Him who sent Me."

Then the seventy returned with joy, saying, "Lord, even the demons are subject to us in Your name."

And He said to them, "I saw Satan fall like lightning from heaven. Behold, I give you the authority to trample on serpents and scorpions, and over all the power of the enemy, and nothing shall by any means hurt you. Nevertheless do not rejoice in this, that the spirits are subject to you, but rather rejoice because your names are written in heaven."

In that hour Jesus rejoiced in the Spirit and said, "I thank You, Father, Lord of heaven and earth, that You have hidden these things from the wise and prudent and revealed them to babes. Even so, Father, for so it seemed good in Your sight. All things have been delivered to Me by My Father, and no one knows who the Son is except the Father, and who the Father is except the Son, and the one to whom the Son wills to reveal Him."

Then He turned to His disciples and said privately, "Blessed are the eyes which see the things you see; for I tell you that many prophets and kings have desired to see what you see, and have not seen it, and to hear what you hear, and have not heard it." (Luke 10:1–24 NKJV)

From Miletus he sent to Ephesus and called for the elders of the church. And when they had come to him, he said to them: "You know, from the first day that I came to Asia, in what manner I always lived among you, serving the Lord with all humility, with many tears and trials which happened to me by the plotting of the Jews; how I kept back nothing that was helpful, but proclaimed it to you, and taught you publicly and from house to house, testifying to Jews, and also to Greeks, repentance toward God and faith toward our Lord Jesus Christ. And see, now I go bound in the spirit to Jerusalem, not knowing the things that will happen to me there, except that the Holy Spirit testifies in every city, saying that chains and tribulations await me. But none of these things move me; nor do I count my life dear to myself, so that I may finish my race with joy, and the ministry which I received from the Lord Jesus, to testify to the gospel of the grace of God.

"And indeed, now I know that you all, among whom I have gone preaching the kingdom of God, will see my face no more. Therefore I testify to you this day that I am innocent of the blood of all men. For I have not shunned to declare to you the whole counsel of God. Therefore take heed to yourselves and to all the flock, among which the Holy Spirit has made you overseers, to shepherd the church of God which He purchased with His own blood. For I know this, that after my departure savage wolves will come in among you, not sparing the flock. Also from among yourselves men will rise up, speaking perverse things, to draw away the disciples after themselves. Therefore watch, and remember that for three years I did not cease to warn everyone night and day with tears.

"So now, brethren, I commend you to God and to the word of His grace, which is able to build you up and give you an inheritance among all those who are sanctified. I have coveted no one's silver or gold or apparel. Yes, you yourselves know that these hands have provided for my necessities, and for those who were with me. I have shown you in every way, by laboring like this, that you must support the weak. And remember the words of the Lord Jesus, that He said, 'It is more blessed to give than to receive.'"

And when he had said these things, he knelt down and prayed with them all. Then they all wept freely, and fell on Paul's neck and kissed him, sorrowing most of all for the words which he spoke, that they would see his face no more. And they accompanied him to the ship. (Acts 20:17–38 NKJV)

Now it came to pass, as He was praying in a certain place, when He ceased, that one of His disciples said to Him, "Lord, teach us to pray, as John also taught his disciples."

So He said to them, "When you pray, say: Our Father in heaven, Hallowed be Your name. Your kingdom come. Your will be done on earth as it is in heaven. Give us day by day our daily bread. And forgive us our sins, for we also forgive everyone who is indebted to us. And do not lead us into temptation, but deliver us from the evil one."

And He said to them, "Which of you shall have a friend, and go to him at midnight and say to him, 'Friend, lend me three loaves; for a friend of mine has come to me on his journey, and I have nothing to set before him'; and he will answer from within and say, 'Do not trouble me; the door is now shut, and my children are with me in bed; I cannot rise and give to you'? I say to you, though he will not rise and give to him because he is his friend, yet because of his persistence he will rise and give him as many as he needs.

"So I say to you, ask, and it will be given to you; seek, and you will find; knock, and it will be opened to you. For everyone who asks receives, and he who seeks finds, and to him who knocks it will be opened. If a son asks for bread from any father among you, will he give him a stone? Or if he asks for a fish, will he give him a serpent instead of a fish? Or if he asks for an egg, will he offer him a scorpion? If you then, being evil, know how to give good gifts to your children, how much more will your heavenly Father give the Holy Spirit to those who ask Him!" (Luke 11:1–13 NKJV)

Discussion (20–30 minutes)

Again, your discussion of these questions is the most important part of the session.

Note to leader: **For the discussion time in this session, it's probably wise to remain together rather than dividing into smaller groups. This session won't call for as much participation from your members, since most of them are probably not gifted as equippers. However, it's critical for your members to understand what qualifies someone to function in an equipping role.**

    1. What is the primary factor in determining if someone is called to be an equipper in the body of Christ?

    2. Do a person's spiritual gifts alone determine his or her role as an equipper?

Note to leader: **In addition to one's gifting, spiritual maturity, godly character, and proven faithfulness are necessary requirements for someone to be an equipper.**

    3. Identify someone in the body of Christ who has been an equipper in your life. (Explain why and how.)

    4. For what reason(s) can the equipping gifts be placed under the broad heading of "leadership" gifts?

    5. What's the difference between a leader who functions as a "trained server" and a leader who functions as a "people equipper"?

    6. What are the three primary tasks of an equipper? What roles do each of the equipping gifts play in accomplishing these tasks?

Application Zone

Below is an assessment called "Your Equipper-Server Quotient." It's helpful in determining the difference between equippers and servers and in evaluating yourself along those lines.

Note to leader: If there's time, take a few minutes to have each member complete this assessment while you are all together. Otherwise, ask each member to complete the assessment before your next meeting together.

Your Equipper-Server Quotient

At this point, it would be good to identify where you see yourself along the equipper-server continuum in several areas.

1. Below are seven pairs of statements labeled "A" and "B." For each pair, determine which statement (A or B) tends to be the truest description of you most of the time, and place a check by it.

    You focus your time and energy on …

    ___ A. training others to meet needs.

    ___ B. meeting needs personally.

    Your *primary* ministry goal is …

    ___ A. to develop others so they can serve successfully.

    ___ B. to be used by the Lord to meet a need in someone's life.

    You think of ministry as an opportunity to …

    ___ A. involve a variety of people to make multiple contributions as a team.

    ___ B. get involved to make your contribution as a team member.

    You're motivated to …

    ___ A. select ministry partners, intentionally hand picking your team members.

    ___ B. involve anyone who's willing to serve.

    You're motivated to …

    ___ A. develop others and delegate the ministry to them.

    ___ B. do the ministry yourself, because then it gets done as you want it to.

    You view ministry …

    ___ A. through "farsighted" lenses—looking to see what will be needed in the future, then raising up or finding the people to expand the team.

___ B. through "nearsighted" lenses—looking to see what's needed now, then acting to accomplish it with the people on the team.

Your most "anointed moments" occur …

    ___ A. when equipping others to carry out God's purposes for their lives.

    ___ B. when you're able to meet a need in someone's life or in the ministry as a whole.

Now add up your selections:

    your number of As: ___

    your number of Bs: ___

    If your score is …

- *7 As, 0 Bs*—you're definitely an equipper.

  Your focus and activities seem to be consistent with other equippers. *Develop your gifts and ministry opportunities in this area.*

- *6 As, 1 B*—you're definitely an equipper.

  Your focus and activities seem to be consistent with other equippers. *Develop your gifts and ministry opportunities in this area.*

- *5 As, 2 Bs*—you're probably an equipper.

  You demonstrated some repeated characteristics that you should explore and further pursue. It indicates some real potential in this area, and you should *seek additional input from leaders and those you minister with.*

- *4 As, 3 Bs*—you're possibly an equipper.

  There were some mild indications in your style and approach of the equipper. Be open to what God might do through your ministry involvements. *Find the kind of ministry positions that will enable you to develop your equipper tendencies for additional clarification and affirmation.*

- *3 As, 4 Bs*—you're possibly a server.

  There are some mild indications in your style and approach matching those of a server. Be open to what God might do through your ministry involvements. *Find the kind of ministry positions that will enable you to develop your server tendencies for additional clarification and affirmation.*

- *2 As, 5 Bs—*you're probably a server.

    You demonstrated some repeated characteristics that you should explore and further pursue. It indicates some real potential in this area, and you should *seek additional input from leaders and those you minister with.*

- *1 A, 6 Bs—*you're definitely a server.

    Your focus and activities seem to be consistent with other servers. *Develop your gifts and ministry opportunities in this area.*

- *0 As, 7 Bs—*you're definitely a server.

    Your focus and activities seem to be consistent with other servers. *Develop your gifts and ministry opportunities in this area.*

Note: Some people tend to rate themselves according to how they think they *should* respond, rather than answering more realistically. This assessment is meant to simply be a guide to help you better identify who God has made you to be and how to more effectively lead and serve accordingly. *The Holy Spirit in you, along with the people you serve with, will provide you with additional feedback and input.*

You need to know if you're primarily an equipper or a server so you can pursue the appropriate kind of ministry role. Each role requires someone with the passion and spiritual gifts that could be summarized as primarily an equipper or a server.

2. For the sake of illustration and discussion, use your A and B scores above to identify to what degree you're either an equipper or server. Based on your score, circle the corresponding percentage on the list below:

    7 As, 0 Bs—100% Equipper

    6 As, 1 B—85% Equipper

    5 As, 2 Bs—70% Equipper

    4 As, 3 Bs—55% Equipper

    3 As, 4 Bs—55% Server

    2 As, 5 Bs—70% Server

    1 A, 6 Bs—85% Server

    0 As, 7 Bs—100% Server

3. You should now have an idea about whether you're primarily an equipper or a server. Now it's time to compare that with an assessment of your current ministry position(s) or role(s), as indicated below.

Identify your current positions or roles (up to three of them) in ministry service; in the spaces indicated below, write a word or two to serve as a label for each one.

For each of these roles or positions, decide what *percentage* of your ministry time and activities tend to fall into each category—*equipping* and *serving*. Write the percentages below. (There are *no* right or wrong responses here! Just use your best estimate.)

A. Position / Role: _____

____ % equipping

____ % serving

B. Position / Role: _____

____ % equipping

____ % serving

C. Position / Role: _____

____ % equipping

____ % serving

Now compare these figures with the answer you circled in question 2 above. Does there seem to be a close match? Check your answers:

Position/Role A: __ *yes* __ *no*

Position/Role B: __ *yes* __ *no*

Position/Role C: __ *yes* __ *no*

What do you feel the Spirit of God is saying to you right now about who you are, the role(s) you're in, and any changes you may need to make? Pray. Listen. Write your thoughts:

Note to leader: **Follow up with your members to discuss whether they see themselves primarily as equippers or as servers. For each person who sees himself or herself as an equipper, it would be wise to get together personally for further discussion about this.**

For Ministry Teams

Note to leader: **In this session, it's important to begin determining which of your team members is gifted for an equipping role (a leadership position). If your team is already well on its way in accurately determining this, the questions below can help you take the next steps.**

However, if it's not yet clear who the equippers and servers are on your team—and, more importantly, if they aren't positioned accordingly—it would be wise to wait until later before discussing these questions. (Session 4 will focus on the role and contribution of servers—those whose primary gifting calls them to the work of service. And session 5 will emphasize the critical importance of positioning equippers in equipping roles and servers in serving roles.)

1. How do the equippers on our team serve to fulfill the three primary tasks mentioned in the DVD teaching?

2. What are the primary responsibilities of the equippers on our team?

3. Think about those who are gifted (and therefore called) to equip. To what degree are they free to focus on equipping instead of feeling responsible to function also as a "trained server"?

4. What changes need to be made on our team to free equippers to function as God intended?

Note to leader: **By the end of this study course, consider giving a copy of the book *Experiencing LeaderShift* to all those in your group who see themselves as equippers. Make plans to lead them together through the *Experiencing LeaderShift Application Guide*. In this way, you're equipping your leaders to lead as God intends them to lead, and you're setting forth a 2 Timothy 2:2 model of ministry instruction.**

Scripture Memory

And He gave some as apostles, and some as prophets, and some as evangelists, and some as pastors, and teachers, for the equipping of the saints for the work of service, to the building up of the body of Christ. (Eph. 4:11–12)

The things which you have heard from me in the presence of many witnesses, entrust these to faithful men who will be able to teach others also. (2 Tim. 2:2)

A pupil is not above his teacher; but everyone, after he has been fully trained, will be like his teacher. (Luke 6:40)

Daily Devotions

Day 1

Read and reflect on Acts 20:17–38.

Here we read again of Paul's final time with the elders from the church at Ephesus. We have good reason to believe Paul had personally chosen these elders, and it's clear, from verses 36–38, that he had a very close relationship with them.

From this passage, list or mark everything you see and hear that would indicate Paul's role as an equipper in the lives of these elders. How does he equip through his example? How does he equip through his instructions to them? Identify everything Paul says and does here related to equipping these elders.

[17] From Miletus he sent to Ephesus and called for the elders of the church. [18] And when they had come to him, he said to them: "You know, from the first day that I came to Asia, in what manner I always lived among you, [19] serving the Lord with all humility, with many tears and trials which happened to me by the plotting of the Jews; [20] how I kept back nothing that was helpful, but proclaimed it to you, and taught you publicly and from house to house, [21] testifying to Jews, and also to Greeks, repentance toward God and faith toward our Lord Jesus Christ. [22] And see, now I go bound in the

spirit to Jerusalem, not knowing the things that will happen to me there, [23] except that the Holy Spirit testifies in every city, saying that chains and tribulations await me. [24] But none of these things move me; nor do I count my life dear to myself, so that I may finish my race with joy, and the ministry which I received from the Lord Jesus, to testify to the gospel of the grace of God.

[25] "And indeed, now I know that you all, among whom I have gone preaching the kingdom of God, will see my face no more. [26] Therefore I testify to you this day that I am innocent of the blood of all men. [27] For I have not shunned to declare to you the whole counsel of God. [28] Therefore take heed to yourselves and to all the flock, among which the Holy Spirit has made you overseers, to shepherd the church of God which He purchased with His own blood. [29] For I know this, that after my departure savage wolves will come in among you, not sparing the flock. [30] Also from among yourselves men will rise up, speaking perverse things, to draw away the disciples after themselves. [31] Therefore watch, and remember that for three years I did not cease to warn everyone night and day with tears.

[32] "So now, brethren, I commend you to God and to the word of His grace, which is able to build you up and give you an inheritance among all those who are sanctified. [33] I have coveted no one's silver or gold or apparel. [34] Yes, you yourselves know that these hands have provided for my necessities, and for those who were with me. [35] I have shown you in every way, by laboring like this, that you must support the weak. And remember the words of the Lord Jesus, that He said, 'It is more blessed to give than to receive.'"

[36] And when he had said these things, he knelt down and prayed with them all. [37] Then they all wept freely, and fell on Paul's neck and kissed him, [38] sorrowing most of all for the words which he spoke, that they would see his face no more. And they accompanied him to the ship. (Acts 20:17–38 NKJV)

Day 2

Read and reflect on these verses.

And He spoke a parable to them: "Can the blind lead the blind? Will they not both fall into the ditch? A disciple is not above his teacher, but everyone who is perfectly trained will be like his teacher." (Luke 6:39–40 NKJV)

Let no one despise your youth, but be an example to the believers in word, in conduct, in love, in spirit, in faith, in purity. (1 Tim. 4:12 NKJV)

And the things that you have heard from me among many witnesses, commit these to faithful men who will be able to teach others also. (2 Tim. 2:2 NKJV)

1. What do each of these verses have to do with equipping?

2. Why is a leader's example so important?

3. What do these verses tell you about who you should follow? (Make your list as complete as you can.)

4. What do these verses tell you about influencing others?

5. Why do you think Paul instructed Timothy to "commit" the things he'd received to "faithful men"?

Day 3

Read and reflect on Luke 10:1–11 again.

In this passage, we see Jesus preparing seventy of His disciples for service.

[1] After these things the Lord appointed seventy others also, and sent them two by two before His face into every city and place where He Himself was about to go. [2] Then He said to them, "The harvest truly is great, but the laborers are few; therefore pray the Lord of the harvest to send out laborers into

His harvest. [3] Go your way; behold, I send you out as lambs among wolves. [4] Carry neither money bag, knapsack, nor sandals; and greet no one along the road. [5] But whatever house you enter, first say, 'Peace to this house.' [6] And if a son of peace is there, your peace will rest on it; if not, it will return to you. [7] And remain in the same house, eating and drinking such things as they give, for the laborer is worthy of his wages. Do not go from house to house. [8] Whatever city you enter, and they receive you, eat such things as are set before you. [9] And heal the sick there, and say to them, 'The kingdom of God has come near to you.' [10] But whatever city you enter, and they do not receive you, go out into its streets and say, [11] 'The very dust of your city which clings to us we wipe off against you. Nevertheless know this, that the kingdom of God has come near you." (Luke 10:1–11 NKJV)

1. Make a list of all that Jesus provides in the way of instruction to prepare these seventy for their service.

2. In what way did His preparation of them have an equipping influence?

3. What lessons did they learn from His instruction that would likely have stayed with them for the rest of their lives?

4. What, if anything, surprises you in these instructions? And what implications would these "surprising" instructions have for you in your current ministry?

_____

Day 4

Read and reflect on Luke 10:17–24, which continues yesterday's passage.

[17] Then the seventy returned with joy, saying, "Lord, even the demons are subject to us in Your name."

[18] And He said to them, "I saw Satan fall like lightning from heaven. [19] Behold, I give you the authority to trample on serpents and scorpions, and over all the power of the enemy, and nothing shall by any means hurt you. [20] Nevertheless do not rejoice in this, that the spirits are subject to you, but rather rejoice because your names are written in heaven."

[21] In that hour Jesus rejoiced in the Spirit and said, "I thank You, Father, Lord of heaven and earth, that You have hidden these things from the wise and prudent and revealed them to babes. Even so, Father, for so it seemed good in Your sight. [22] All things have been delivered to Me by My Father, and no one knows who the Son is except the Father, and who the Father is except the Son, and the one to whom the Son wills to reveal Him."

[23] Then He turned to His disciples and said privately, "Blessed are the eyes which see the things you see; [24] for I tell you that many prophets and kings have desired to see what you see, and have not seen it, and to hear what you hear, and have not heard it." (Luke 10:17–24 NKJV)

1. What had occurred in the experience of the Seventy that caused them to return "with joy" (v. 17)?

2. What do we learn about spiritual warfare from verses 18–19?

3. In verse 20, what does Jesus tell them should be the real cause for joy? Why is this true?

4. In verses 21–22, what reasons does Jesus give for praising His Father?

5. When Jesus says, "Blessed are the eyes which see the things you see" (vv. 23–24), what is He referring to?

6. What do you learn about Jesus and about serving Him from this passage?

Day 5

Read and reflect on 2 Timothy 4:1–8.

In these verses, Paul gives one last exhortation to Timothy, his son in the faith. Paul had equipped Timothy for ministry leadership, and this passage is one final example of this equipping.

¹ I charge you therefore before God and the Lord Jesus Christ, who will judge the living and the dead at His appearing and His kingdom: ² Preach the word! Be ready in season and out of season. Convince, rebuke, exhort, with all longsuffering and teaching. ³ For the time will come when they will not endure sound doctrine, but according to their own desires, because they have itching ears, they will heap up for themselves teachers; ⁴ and they will turn their ears away from the truth, and be turned aside to fables. ⁵ But you be watchful in all things, endure afflictions, do the work of an evangelist, fulfill your ministry.

⁶ For I am already being poured out as a drink offering, and the time of my departure is at hand. ⁷ I have fought the good fight, I have finished the race, I have kept the faith. ⁸ Finally, there is laid up for me the crown of righteousness, which the Lord, the righteous Judge, will give to me on that Day, and not to me only but also to all who have loved His appearing. (2 Tim. 4:1–8 NKJV)

1. Make a list of the points of instruction Paul gives here to equip Timothy for ministry leadership.

2. What does Paul provide by way of example to help equip Timothy for leadership?

3. What does this final exhortation tell us about the nature of Paul's relationship with Timothy?

4. What can we learn from this passage? What implications does it have for your life and ministry?

5. If you were to write a final exhortation to three of your followers, what would your primary messages be?

6. When you reach the end of your life, what final words would you like to say as you reflect upon your time on earth?

SESSION 4

THE SERVER

For the Leader

While *Experiencing LeaderShift* is written primarily for leaders, it contains foundational truth that relates to every follower of Jesus Christ. Having a biblical perspective on serving the Lord is fundamental to serving in the right way for the right reasons. In *Experiencing LeaderShift,* you'll find the content of chapter 4 ("The Serving Heresy") and chapter 8 ("The Blessing Factor") to be especially helpful in this regard. We strongly encourage you to review these chapters so your thinking aligns with Scripture as you lead this session.

Objectives

While some are gifted by the Holy Spirit for the work of equipping, many others are gifted for the work of service. We call these people *servers.* They serve on the frontlines of ministry, meeting needs. Their service may be either task-focused or people-focused.

In this session, we'll look more closely at the role of servers in the body of Christ. This session has four primary objectives:

1. To bring further clarification regarding the difference between equippers and servers. While none of us is completely one or the other, by gifting we're primarily either an equipper or a server.
2. To help each member clearly understand whether he or she is primarily an equipper or a server.

3. To recognize the esteemed value of servers and to affirm their critical role in the body of Christ.

4. To give servers a vision for what it means to be on the frontlines of what God is accomplishing through His church in our world.

Icebreaker (optional; 5–8 minutes)

Again, refer to the icebreaker suggestions in the "For Leaders Only" section at the front of this Leader's Guide.

Prayer Together

As an opening prayer, ask God to enlighten all of you regarding His calling for your lives.

> I pray that the eyes of your heart may be enlightened, so that you will know what is the hope of His calling, what are the riches of the glory of His inheritance in the saints, and what is the surpassing greatness of His power toward us who believe. These are in accordance with the working of the strength of His might. (Eph. 1:18–19)

The end of this week's session would be a great time to pray over each person with serving gifts. You can do this in smaller groups or all together, depending on the number of members.

Learning Together

Note to leader: **This content is included in the Participant's Guide (starting on page 89)—except for text in bold (like this), which is for you as the leader.**

Introduction

Note to leader: **Have someone read this aloud.**

Whether it's at a restaurant, a car repair shop, a retail store, or on the phone, we've all had memorable experiences with "customer service"—some positive, others negative. Because of the impact customer service has on the average consumer, companies of every kind devote lots of attention in striving for outstanding customer service.

God also understands the importance of customer service. As a result, He gifts certain members of His body in such a way that they stand on the frontlines offering service. These members become the hands and feet, the heart and mind, and the mouth, eyes, and ears of God Himself to those in need. Whether it's a word of encouragement, an act of mercy, or the warmth of hospitality, service on God's behalf brings His resources to meet a need.

In this session, we'll look at the role of servers in the body of Christ. These are the people among us who stand on the frontlines of ministry as God's agents of "customer service." When they serve as they're called, the body functions as God intended, and everyone benefits.

Warm-up Questions (10 minutes)
Answering these questions can help everyone sense the importance of "customer service."

1. Can you think of a recent example of outstanding customer service? Explain what happened and what impact this experience had on you.

2. Can you think of a bad customer-service experience you've had? What took place, and what impact did this experience have on you?

3. Make a list of the characteristics of outstanding customer service.

DVD Teaching (14 minutes)
Watch the DVD teaching segment for session 4, jotting down a few notes as you do.

This teaching segment presents these five primary points:

1. The Holy Spirit distributes spiritual gifts to members of the body for the express purpose of meeting needs in someone else's life or in the body as a whole.

2. Every member of the body has at least one spiritual gift and therefore has a role to play in the body.

3. It's critical that those with serving gifts be positioned to carry out works of service in keeping with their gifts.

4. No one is only an equipper or only a server. To some degree, we're all both. However, based on the spiritual gifts we possess, we have a *primary* role as one or the other.

5. Equippers and servers think and function differently, as seen in some characteristic differences.

Key Bible Passage

While Ephesians 4:12 provides us with the overarching truth that members of the body of Christ are to carry out the work of service, Romans 12:4–10 gives us specific examples of how this work of service is carried out, based on giftedness.

As you go through this passage, think of specific examples in your church of what's mentioned there.

[4] For just as we have many members in one body and all the members do not have the same function,

[5] so we, who are many, are one body in Christ, and individually members one of another.

⁶ Since we have gifts that differ according to the grace given to us, *each of us is to exercise them accordingly*: if prophecy, according to the proportion of his faith; ⁷ if service, in his serving; or he who teaches, in his teaching; ⁸ or he who exhorts, in his exhortation; he who gives, with liberality; he who leads, with diligence; he who shows mercy, with cheerfulness.

⁹ Let love be without hypocrisy. Abhor what is evil; cling to what is good.

¹⁰ Be devoted to one another in brotherly love; give preference to one another in honor.

Notes on this passage for the leader:
Verse 4—**Many members, many different functions.**
Verse 5—**Many members, joined to one another in one body.**
Verses 6–8—**We have different gifts. Each of us is to exercise the gift(s) we've been given.**
Verse 9—**Be genuine in the expression of your gift. Don't simply go through the motions.**
Verse 10—**Put one another ahead of self. In a word—SERVE!**

Discussion (20–30 minutes)

Again, your discussion of these questions is the most important part of the session.

1. Below is a list of "serving gifts" mentioned in the New Testament. For each one, describe *who* is on the receiving end of the service and the *need* being met through the exercise of this serving gift.

gift	recipient	need met
mercy		
helps		
giving		
administration		

hospitality

intercession

discernment

encouragement

faith

healing

interpretation

knowledge

miracles

tongues

wisdom

creative
  communication

craftsmanship

2. Identify a recent, real-life example of a serving gift at work.

3. Name two or three people who you see as clearly having primary gifts of a serving nature. What causes you to draw this conclusion about them?

4. In what ways was Jesus a server?

5. In what ways is your church or ministry strong in the expression of serving gifts?

6. In what ways is your church or ministry lacking in the expression of serving gifts?

What serving gifts appear to be in short supply?

For Ministry Teams

1. Who are the primary "customers" of our ministry?

2. What needs do they have that, to be met, require us to use our gifts?

3. Which serving gifts are most needed on our ministry team to meet these needs?

4. Is there a need for additional serving gifts on our team? Which ones? What could we do as a team to bring people with these gifts into our ministry?

Application Zone

Application / Assessment

For your next session together, be prepared to briefly share what you believe your role is in the body of Christ. Use these questions to help shape what you share:

1. What do you believe to be your primary spiritual gifts?

2. As a result of this study and the group's discussion, has anything changed in your understanding of your spiritual gifts? If so, what?

3. What role do you see yourself playing as a result of having these gifts?

4. What contribution will you commit yourself to making for the common good?

Note to leader: **Emphasize the importance and helpfulness of this assignment. Don't think of it as optional.**

Scripture Memory

Be devoted to one another in brotherly love; give preference to one another in honor. (Rom. 12:10)

But to each one is given the manifestation of the Spirit for the common good. (1 Cor. 12:7)

For you were called to freedom, brethren; only do not turn your freedom into an opportunity for the flesh, but through love serve one another. (Gal. 5:13)

Daily Devotions

___

Day 1

Read and reflect on Matthew 10:1–15.

[1] And when He had called His twelve disciples to Him, He gave them power over unclean spirits, to cast them out, and to heal all kinds of sickness and all kinds of disease. [2] Now the names of the twelve apostles are these: first, Simon, who is called Peter, and Andrew his brother; James the son of Zebedee, and John his brother; [3] Philip and Bartholomew; Thomas and Matthew the tax collector; James the son of Alphaeus, and Lebbaeus, whose surname was Thaddaeus; [4] Simon the Cananite, and Judas Iscariot, who also betrayed Him.

⁵ These twelve Jesus sent out and commanded them, saying: "Do not go into the way of the Gentiles, and do not enter a city of the Samaritans. ⁶ But go rather to the lost sheep of the house of Israel. ⁷ And as you go, preach, saying, 'The kingdom of heaven is at hand.' ⁸ Heal the sick, cleanse the lepers, raise the dead, cast out demons. Freely you have received, freely give. ⁹ Provide neither gold nor silver nor copper in your money belts, ¹⁰ nor bag for your journey, nor two tunics, nor sandals, nor staffs; for a worker is worthy of his food.

¹¹ "Now whatever city or town you enter, inquire who in it is worthy, and stay there till you go out. ¹² And when you go into a household, greet it. ¹³ If the household is worthy, let your peace come upon it. But if it is not worthy, let your peace return to you. ¹⁴ And whoever will not receive you nor hear your words, when you depart from that house or city, shake off the dust from your feet. ¹⁵ Assuredly, I say to you, it will be more tolerable for the land of Sodom and Gomorrah in the day of judgment than for that city!" (Matt. 10:1–15 NKJV)

1. Jesus gave His twelve disciples "authority" (v. 1). In what ways has God given us authority concerning the work of His kingdom?

2. What did this authority enable the twelve disciples to do (v. 1)?

3. What does *your* "authority" enable you to do?

4. Considering the power and authority the disciples were able to display, what enabled them to see themselves as servants?

5. How did other people benefit from the ministry of the disciples? How do you think they responded?

6. What can you learn from this passage about your own participation in the work of service?

Day 2

Read and reflect on Mark 2:1–13.

[1] And again He entered Capernaum after some days, and it was heard that He was in the house. [2] Immediately many gathered together, so that there was no longer room to receive them, not even near the door. And He preached the word to them. [3] Then they came to Him, bringing a paralytic who was carried by four men. [4] And when they could not come near Him because of the crowd, they uncovered the roof where He was. So when they had broken through, they let down the bed on which the paralytic was lying.

[5] When Jesus saw their faith, He said to the paralytic, "Son, your sins are forgiven you."

[6] And some of the scribes were sitting there and reasoning in their hearts, [7] "Why does this Man speak blasphemies like this? Who can forgive sins but God alone?"

[8] But immediately, when Jesus perceived in His spirit that they reasoned thus within themselves, He said to them, "Why do you reason about these things in your hearts? [9] Which is easier, to say to the paralytic, 'Your sins are forgiven you,' or to say, 'Arise, take up your bed and walk'? [10] But that you may know that the Son of Man has power on earth to forgive sins"—He said to the paralytic, [11] "I say to you, arise, take up your bed, and go to your house." [12] Immediately he arose, took up the bed, and went out in the presence of them all, so that all were amazed and glorified God, saying, "We never saw anything like this!"

[13] Then He went out again by the sea; and all the multitude came to Him, and He taught them. (Mark 2:1–13 NKJV)

1. Why do you suppose such a large crowd gathered at this home in Capernaum (vv. 1–2)?

2. What can we reasonably conclude about the four men who brought the paralytic to Jesus (vv. 3–4)?

3. What were the chances that the paralytic would have been healed had his friends not carried him to Jesus? What's the significance of that for us?

4. Why did the scribes become upset with what Jesus said and did (vv. 6–7)?

5. When Jesus healed this man, how did the people respond (vv. 12–13)?

6. In what ways was Jesus a server?

7. What can you learn from this episode about serving others?

Day 3

Read and reflect on the following passages.

[14] Then Jesus returned in the power of the Spirit to Galilee, and news of Him went out through all the surrounding region. [15] And He taught in their synagogues, being glorified by all.

[16] So He came to Nazareth, where He had been brought up. And as His custom was, He went into the synagogue on the Sabbath day, and stood up to read. [17] And He was handed the book of the prophet Isaiah. And when He had opened the book, He found the place where it was written:

[18] "The Spirit of the LORD is upon Me,

Because He has anointed Me

To preach the gospel to the poor;

He has sent Me to heal the brokenhearted,

To proclaim liberty to the captives

And recovery of sight to the blind,

To set at liberty those who are oppressed;

[19] To proclaim the acceptable year of the LORD."

[20] Then He closed the book, and gave it back to the attendant and sat down. And the eyes of all who were in the synagogue were fixed on Him. (Luke 4:14–20 NKJV)

Then James and John, the sons of Zebedee, came to Him, saying, "Teacher, we want You to do for us whatever we ask." (Mark 10:35 NKJV)

How God anointed Jesus of Nazareth with the Holy Spirit and with power, who went about doing good and healing all who were oppressed by the devil, for God was with Him. (Acts 10:38 NKJV)

Make a list of everything we can learn about serving from these passages. Consider …
—what Jesus did.

—what He taught.

—what He said about Himself.

—what Peter said about Him.

—what Peter said about His influence.

—why Jesus came.

—who He came to serve.

—how He served.

What impact does your list have on you?

Day 4

Read and reflect on Philippians 2:25–30.

²⁵ Yet I considered it necessary to send to you Epaphroditus, my brother, fellow worker, and fellow soldier, but your messenger and the one who ministered to my need; ²⁶ since he was longing for you all, and was distressed because you had heard that he was sick. ²⁷ For indeed he was sick almost unto death; but God had mercy on him, and not only on him but on me also, lest I should have sorrow upon sorrow. ²⁸ Therefore I sent him the more eagerly, that when you see him again you may rejoice, and I may be less sorrowful. ²⁹ Receive him therefore in the Lord with all gladness, and hold such men in esteem; ³⁰ because for the work of Christ he came close to death, not regarding his life, to supply what was lacking in your service toward me. (Phil. 2:25–30 NKJV)

1. In verse 25, Paul uses these terms to describe Epaphroditus: "my brother and fellow worker and fellow soldier." What does this say about Paul's opinion of Epaphroditus?

2. Paul also describes Epaphroditus as a "messenger" from the Philippians and as a "minister to my need" (v. 25). Why do you think this was important to Paul?

3. What can you conclude about Epaphroditus based on what Paul says of him in verse 26?

4. Based on Paul's words in verse 27, how do you think Paul felt about Epaphroditus? Why would he feel this way?

5. How was Paul serving Epaphroditus through what he wrote in these verses?

6. What are the implications for your life and relationships based on what you read here about Paul and Epaphroditus?

Day 5

Read and reflect on Philippians 2:1–11.

¹ Therefore if there is any consolation in Christ, if any comfort of love, if any fellowship of the Spirit, if any affection and mercy, ² fulfill my joy by being like-minded, having the same love, being of one accord, of one mind. ³ Let nothing be done through selfish ambition or conceit, but in lowliness of mind let each esteem others better than himself. ⁴ Let each of you look out not only for his own interests, but also for the interests of others.

⁵ Let this mind be in you which was also in Christ Jesus, ⁶ who, being in the form of God, did not consider it robbery to be equal with God, ⁷ but made Himself of no reputation, taking the form of a bondservant, and coming in the likeness of men. ⁸ And being found in appearance as a man, He

humbled Himself and became obedient to the point of death, even the death of the cross. [9] Therefore God also has highly exalted Him and given Him the name which is above every name, [10] that at the name of Jesus every knee should bow, of those in heaven, and of those on earth, and of those under the earth, [11] and that every tongue should confess that Jesus Christ is Lord, to the glory of God the Father. (Phil. 2:1–11 NKJV)

1. What does Paul's encouragement in verses 1 and 2 have to do with being a servant to others?

2. Why is it so difficult to practice what Paul writes in verses 3–4?

3. Can you think of two or three ways you could apply the exhortation in verses 3–4? (Be specific and practical.)

4. According to verses 6–8, how did Jesus model what Paul wrote in verses 3–4?

5. How did God honor His Son for His act of service (vv. 9–11)?

6. What can you do to apply Philippians 2:1–11 this week?

SESSION 5

WHY WE NEED TO GET IT RIGHT

For the Leader

This session is tied most closely to the content of chapter 6 ("The Organizational Heresy") in *Experiencing LeaderShift*. When the church functions as an institution, everyone loses (fails). You may want to reread that chapter to refresh your understanding of the church's structure and function.

Objectives

From Christ's words in John 15, we see that it is God's will that we bear fruit—*much* fruit, in fact—for His glory. To this end, God "prunes" us so we "may bear more fruit."

God doesn't want anything to get in the way of our success (as biblically defined). He wants us to be incredibly successful—faithful, fruitful, and fulfilled in a way that makes Him famous.

In this session, we'll take a hard, honest look at some of the obstacles to personal success and ministry effectiveness. This session has four primary objectives:

1. To provide answers for some important questions commonly asked about equippers and servers.

2. To provide further wisdom and understanding about equippers and servers that will remove obstacles to personal success and ministry effectiveness.

3. To better understand God's intention for the way churches and ministries should be organized.

4. *(If you're a ministry team leader:)* To give you the information you need to address the proper placement of each member of your ministry team.

Icebreaker *(optional; 5–8 minutes)*

At this point in *Experiencing LeaderShift Together,* it's probably wise to use an icebreaker that allows everyone in the group to affirm and encourage one another—and thereby receive encouragement and affirmation as well. We all need this, yet we seldom take the time or make the effort to provide it.

You could ask group members to

   —*share something they've come to appreciate about someone else (such as the person on their right) as a result of being in this group/team together.*

   —*choose one or two words that best describe what they've come to respect about one of their fellow members.*

   —*identify where they can clearly see God's hand upon the life and ministry of that person.*

Or come up with your own questions and activities that will promote the most encouragement and affirmation for your members.

Prayer Together

You may want to ask everyone to focus on giving thanks for each other—especially for one another's specific gifting from God and the contributions each person has made in serving within the body of Christ.

Learning Together

Note to leader: **This content is included in the Participant's Guide (starting on page 105)—except for text in bold (like this), which is for you as the leader.**

Introduction

Note to leader: **Have someone read this aloud.**

The apostle Paul wrote a letter we know as 1 Corinthians to address a number of issues hindering the growth of the believers in Corinth. In some cases, they made mistakes due to ignorance or immaturity.

In others, their mistakes were due to disobedience.

Whatever the cause, the consequences were deeply felt. The church lacked unity. Members were engaged in sinful practices that hindered their fellowship with God and one another. Their testimony before the unbelieving community was a poor one, and their influence was minimal.

Paul writes this letter to address their ignorance, immaturity, and disobedience. In chapter 14 in particular, he addresses errors in their thinking and mistakes in their practices that were particularly damaging to their success and unity as a body. While this hard-hitting letter must have stung a few people, the changes brought about in response to Paul's instruction surely yielded a fruit of blessing.

Times and issues have changed to some degree since Paul wrote, but the principles used to address such issues have not. The principles that enable the body of Christ to function in unity are timeless.

In this session, we want to look at some of these fundamental principles. We'll try to answer some commonly asked questions about equippers and servers. We also want to address some common mistakes that hinder personal success and ministry effectiveness.

Remember, it's God's will that you be incredibly successful as *He* defines success (being faithful, bearing fruit, and experiencing fulfillment in a way that makes Him famous). It's also His will that the church or ministry you're involved in be incredibly effective in accomplishing His purposes.

Warm-up Questions (10 minutes)

Answering these questions can help everyone sense the impact of doing something the wrong way.

1. Can you think of a time and place in your life (at work, school, church, etc.) when a lack of information or your lack of proper understanding hindered your success? Explain.

2. Can you think of a time when you thought or functioned in a way that hindered your fellowship with God or others? Explain.

DVD Teaching (17 minutes)

Watch the DVD teaching segment for session 5, taking notes as you listen.

This session's teaching brings out several points:

1. Six commonly asked questions about equippers and servers:

—   Does everyone start out in ministry as a server? *(Yes.)*

—   Can anyone start out in ministry as an equipper? *(No.)*

—   What's involved in a person becoming an equipper? *(Equipping gifts, spiritual maturity, godly character, and proven faithfulness.)*

—   Do we choose our primary role? *(No, the Holy Spirit does.)*

—   Was Jesus an equipper or a server? *(He was both.)*

—   Can a person develop into an equipper? *(Yes—although such development is a reflection of giftedness, not a mark of spiritual maturity.)*

2. Four common errors related to equippers and servers:

Error 1: Those with primary serving gifts are placed in equipping roles (such as Marty in the DVD).

Error 2: Those with primary equipping gifts are placed in serving roles.

Error 3: Those who are gifted to equip function as "trained servers" (such as the pastor who becomes the primary "need-meeter" in the church).

Error 4: Those in equipping roles function as "skilled users."

3. Some characteristic differences between an equipper and a "user":

Equippers relate to give.

> *Users relate to get.*

Equippers focus on those they lead.

> *Users focus on end results; those they lead are a means to that end.*

Equippers invest in their followers.

> *Users invest in followers who produce the most results.*

Equippers receive fulfillment from the success of their followers.

> *Users receive fulfillment from ministry success (usually numerically defined success).*

Equippers value the person.

Users value the person's contribution; therefore a person becomes expendable if he or she fails to make a valued contribution.

Equippers develop a loyal following.

Users cycle through followers.

4. The equipper paradigm:

> *Jesus the Equipper* → *"used"* → *the ministry*
> → *to equip* → *His disciples.*

5. Those in leadership positions should function as equippers.

6. Those gifted to serve should focus on the work of service.

7. Let your role reflect who God made you to be.

Key Bible Passage

In 1 Corinthians 14 we find a good example of what happens when the body fails to function as God intended—plus the right way to respond to that deficiency.

Note to leader: As time permits, walk through some of the main lessons from this chapter. You may also want to encourage your group members to study the chapter as a part of their daily devotions that follow this session.

[1] Pursue love, yet desire earnestly spiritual gifts, but especially that you may prophesy. [2] For one who speaks in a tongue does not speak to men but to God; for no one understands, but in his spirit he speaks mysteries. [3] But one who prophesies speaks to men for edification and exhortation and consolation.

[4] One who speaks in a tongue edifies himself; but one who prophesies edifies the church. [5] Now I wish that you all spoke in tongues, but even more that you would prophesy; and greater is one who prophesies than one who speaks in tongues, unless he interprets, so that the church may receive edifying.

[6] But now, brethren, if I come to you speaking in tongues, what will I profit you unless I speak to you either by way of revelation or of knowledge or of prophecy or of teaching? [7] Yet even lifeless things, either flute or harp, in producing a sound, if they do not produce a distinction in the tones, how will it be known what is played on the flute or on the harp? [8] For if the bugle produces an indistinct sound, who will prepare himself for battle? [9] So also you, unless you utter by the tongue speech that is clear, how will it be known what is spoken? For you will be speaking into the air. [10] There are, perhaps, a great many kinds of languages in the world, and no kind is without meaning. [11] If then I do not know the meaning of the language, I will be to the one who speaks a barbarian, and the one who speaks will be a barbarian to me. [12] So also you, since you are zealous of spiritual gifts, seek to abound for the edification of the church.

[13] Therefore let one who speaks in a tongue pray that he may interpret. [14] For if I pray in a tongue, my spirit prays, but my mind is unfruitful. [15] What is the outcome then? I will pray with the spirit and I will pray with the mind also; I will sing with the spirit and I will sing with the mind also. [16] Otherwise if you bless in the spirit only, how will the one who fills the place of the ungifted say the "Amen" at your giving of thanks, since he does not know what you are saying? [17] For you are giving thanks well enough, but the other person is not edified. [18] I thank God, I speak in tongues more than you all; [19] however, in the church I desire to speak five words with my mind so that I may instruct others also, rather than ten thousand words in a tongue. (1 Cor. 14:1–19)

Notes on this passage for the leader: **The following verses highlight some of the errors being made by the believers in Corinth.**

Verses 1–4—**Tongues versus prophecy. What appears to be happening in the Corinthian church, and why?**

Verse 12—**What overall purpose does Paul emphasize here?**

Verses 18–19—**Speaking in a way that blesses others is of greater value than speaking in a way to bless oneself.**

Verse 20—**How is Paul characterizing the believers in Corinth, based on what we read in this verse?**

Verses 22–32—**Guidelines for the expression of prophetic gifting.**

Verses 33, 39–40—God is not a God of confusion; therefore let all things be done in an orderly fashion.

Discussion (20–30 minutes)

Again, your discussion of these questions is the most important part of the session.

1. What do you see as the implications of a person who's primarily gifted as a server functioning in an equipping role?

Note to leader: When servers are in equipping roles, typically they see the need and focus on meeting it, but they (a) don't have a vision for the ministry long-term and (b) don't focus on equipping others.

2. What are the implications of an equipper functioning in a serving role?

Note to leader: Equippers who are in serving roles often seem critical, because they have a vision for how to equip a team, but don't see that vision being accomplished. This is especially true when the person in the leadership position is by gifting a server. They can then become a thorn in the flesh of this "server" leader.

3. What does it mean for an equipper (in an equipping position) to function as a trained server? What are the implications of this for a leader in the ministry?

4. Can you think of someone who fills an equipping position but functions as a trained server?

5. Have you ever been under the leadership of a "user" in any setting?

6. Have you ever been under the leadership of a true equipper? If so, describe your experience.

7. Using a scale of 1 to 10, to what degree are you currently in a role that fits your primary giftedness? ___ (1 = a misfit; 10 = a match made in heaven)

Note to leader: If you haven't done so already, consider giving a copy of the book *Experiencing LeaderShift* to all those in your group who see themselves as equippers. Encourage them to read it; then make arrangements to lead them through the *Experiencing LeaderShift Application Guide*. As the leader, this is a 2 Timothy 2:2 opportunity for you.

For Ministry Teams
Consider the implications of this session's content for your team.

Why is it important for *our particular team* that equippers be involved in equipping, and servers in serving?

Note to leader: As you think through these implications, address potentially needed changes individually with your team members. You may have a server in an equipping role or an equipper in a serving role. You may have an equipper functioning as a trained server or leading with a "user" motivation. It would be wise for you to deal with such situations personally and individually, rather than in front of the entire team.

Application Zone

Application / Assessment
If you're an equipper, compare the following motivational characteristics with your own motivation.

Characteristics of Equippers and Users

In the following list, underline or check the phrases that most accurately describe you.

    Equippers relate to servers in order to *give* them something.

        Users relate to servers in order to *get* something from them.

    Equippers are able to create a loyal following.

Users cycle through servers.

Equippers cause those they lead to feel loved, valued, and appreciated for who they are.

Users cause those they lead to feel "used," sometimes to the point of being resentful. They feel they're valued to the degree that they make a valued contribution.

Equippers see servers (those they lead in the work of the ministry) as the focus of their personal ministry. These servers receive their greatest attention and energy.

Users see the ministry "program" as the focus of their ministry. The programs, events, and activities receive their greatest attention and energy.

Equippers see the servers they lead as an end result of their ministry.

Users see the servers they lead as a means to an end (the *end* being a program's numerical growth).

Equippers see the ministry programs, events, and activities as vehicles to develop the servers they lead.

Users see the servers they lead as a vehicle to get the ministry programs, events, and activities carried out.

Equippers invest in those who serve under their leadership.

Users invest primarily in those servers who make the greatest contribution to the ministry.

Equippers derive their greatest satisfaction from the "success" of those they're leading.

Users derive their greatest satisfaction from the results being achieved in the ministry. Increasing attendance is usually a major motivation, as it signals "success."

Equippers see people and their relationship with them as what is of value.

Users see people and their relationship with them as expendable if they're not making a valued contribution to the ministry.

Equippers measure ministry success in terms of the process as well as the product. How we achieved the results is as important as the results themselves.

Users' success is measured in terms of the "end product" results of the ministry— usually in terms of *nickels* and *noses*.

Equippers very seldom need to use their position of authority to accomplish ministry objectives. Those they lead value their authenticity, their vulnerability, and their humility and trust their heart for them and the ministry.

Users need to exercise force and authority in order to accomplish ministry objectives. They have a tendency to be controlling in their leadership.

Scripture Memory

What is the outcome then, brethren? When you assemble, each one has a psalm, has a teaching, has a revelation, has a tongue, has an interpretation. Let all things be done for edification. (1 Cor. 14:26)

If I speak with the tongues of men and of angels, but do not have love, I have become a noisy gong or a clanging cymbal. And if I have the gift of prophecy, and know all mysteries and all knowledge; and if I have all faith, so as to remove mountains, but do not have love, I am nothing. And if I give all my possessions to feed the poor, and if I surrender my body to be burned, but do not have love, it profits me nothing. (1 Cor. 13:1–3)

Daily Devotions

Day 1
Read and reflect on 1 Corinthians 13:1–13.

¹ If I speak with the tongues of men and of angels, but do not have love, I have become a noisy gong or a clanging cymbal. ² And if I have the gift of prophecy, and know all mysteries and all knowledge; and if I have all faith, so as to remove mountains, but do not have love, I am nothing. ³ And if I give all my possessions to feed the poor, and if I surrender my body to be burned, but do not have love, it profits me nothing.

⁴ Love is patient, love is kind and is not jealous; love does not brag and is not arrogant, ⁵ does not act unbecomingly; it does not seek its own, is not provoked, does not take into account a wrong suffered, ⁶ does not rejoice in unrighteousness, but rejoices with the truth; ⁷ bears all things, believes all things, hopes all things, endures all things.

⁸ Love never fails; but if there are gifts of prophecy, they will be done away; if there are tongues, they will cease; if there is knowledge, it will be done away. ⁹ For we know in part and we prophesy

in part; [10] but when the perfect comes, the partial will be done away. [11] When I was a child, I used to speak like a child, think like a child, reason like a child; when I became a man, I did away with childish things. [12] For now we see in a mirror dimly, but then face to face; now I know in part, but then I shall know fully just as I also have been fully known. [13] But now faith, hope, love, abide these three; but the greatest of these is love. (1 Cor. 13:1–13)

1. Why do you think love is held up with such importance in verses 1–3?

2. From verses 4–8, make a list of what love is. Put these descriptive characteristics in your own words so you clearly understand these characteristics.

3. Identify one or two of these characteristics that are the most difficult for you to express.

4. Think of one or two tangible ways you could currently express this kind of love, and write them here.

5. What is Paul referring to when he speaks of "childish things" (v. 11)? What would the truth of verse 11 mean for you?

_____

Day 2

Read and reflect on 1 Corinthians 14:1–19 (it's included earlier in this session's "Key Bible Passage" section).

1. What do you believe it means to "pursue love" (v. 1)?

2. Why does Paul tell the believers at Corinth to "desire earnestly spiritual gifts," especially the gift of prophecy (v. 1)?

3. What is the purpose of the gift of prophecy (v. 3)?

4. Why does Paul say the gift of prophecy is more profitable than speaking in tongues (v. 4)?

5. Why did God give us spiritual gifts (v. 12)?

6. In what ways is the body of Christ being edified as you use your gift(s)?

Day 3

Read and reflect on 1 Corinthians 14:20–40.

20 Brethren, do not be children in your thinking; yet in evil be infants, but in your thinking be mature. 21 In the Law it is written, "By men of strange tongues and by the lips of strangers I will speak to this people, and even so they will not listen to Me," says the Lord. 22 So then tongues are for a sign, not to those who believe but to unbelievers; but prophecy is for a sign, not to unbelievers but to those who believe. 23 Therefore if the whole church assembles together and all speak in tongues, and ungifted men or unbelievers enter, will they not say that you are mad? 24 But if all prophesy, and an unbeliever or an ungifted man enters, he is convicted by all, he is called to account by all; 25 the secrets of his heart are disclosed; and so he will fall on his face and worship God, declaring that God is certainly among you.

²⁶ What is the outcome then, brethren? When you assemble, each one has a psalm, has a teaching, has a revelation, has a tongue, has an interpretation. Let all things be done for edification. ²⁷ If anyone speaks in a tongue, it should be by two or at the most three, and each in turn, and one must interpret; ²⁸ but if there is no interpreter, he must keep silent in the church; and let him speak to himself and to God. ²⁹ Let two or three prophets speak, and let the others pass judgment. ³⁰ But if a revelation is made to another who is seated, the first one must keep silent. ³¹ For you can all prophesy one by one, so that all may learn and all may be exhorted; ³² and the spirits of prophets are subject to prophets; ³³ for God is not a God of confusion but of peace, as in all the churches of the saints....

³⁷ If anyone thinks he is a prophet or spiritual, let him recognize that the things which I write to you are the Lord's commandment. ³⁸ But if anyone does not recognize this, he is not recognized.

³⁹ Therefore, my brethren, desire earnestly to prophesy, and do not forbid to speak in tongues. ⁴⁰ But all things must be done properly and in an orderly manner. (1 Cor. 14:20–33, 37–40)

1. How would you summarize the purposes stated here (in vv. 20–25) for the gifts of tongues and prophecy?

2. Why do you suppose the gifts of tongues and prophecy are not expressed in some churches today, while they seem to be strongly emphasized in others?

3. State in your own words the instruction Paul gives in verse 26. What is the implication of this truth for you? What is the implication for the body of believers in general?

4. What guidelines does Paul spell out for speaking in tongues and prophecy in verses 27–32?

5. What do you suppose was happening in the Corinthian church that caused Paul to write what he does in verses 33 and 40?

6. In what ways, if any, do you experience confusion or a lack of orderliness in your church or ministry today? How does this situation relate to what you've learned in session 5 of this study?

Day 4
Read and reflect on 1 Corinthians 3:1–8.

[1] And I, brethren, could not speak to you as to spiritual men, but as to men of flesh, as to infants in Christ. [2] I gave you milk to drink, not solid food; for you were not yet able to receive it. Indeed, even now you are not yet able, [3] for you are still fleshly. For since there is jealousy and strife among you, are you not fleshly, and are you not walking like mere men? [4] For when one says, "I am of Paul," and another, "I am of Apollos," are you not mere men?

[5] What then is Apollos? And what is Paul? Servants through whom you believed, even as the Lord gave opportunity to each one. [6] I planted, Apollos watered, but God was causing the growth. [7] So then neither the one who plants nor the one who waters is anything, but God who causes the growth. [8] Now he who plants and he who waters are one; but each will receive his own reward according to his own labor. (1 Cor. 3:1–8)

1. What must have been true of the believers at Corinth for Paul to write, "I could not speak to you as to spiritual men, but as to men of flesh, as to infants in Christ" (v. 1)?

2. What does Paul mean by "I gave you milk to drink, not solid food" (v. 2)? What's the difference? Can you think of specific examples?

3. What evidence do you see that the Corinthians were "fleshly"?

4. How does Paul view himself, and how does he view Apollos (vv. 5–7)?

5. How does this passage apply to you?

6. What is the implication for you in the last part of verse 8: "Each will receive his own reward according to his own labor"?

Day 5

In your Bible, look up 1 Corinthians 4:1–21, and read and reflect on this passage.

1. How does Paul define himself and his fellow ministry workers in verse 1?

2. What does it mean to be "servants of Christ" and "stewards of the mysteries of God" (v. 1)?

3. What does it mean to be "found trustworthy" (v. 2)? Why is this required from a steward?

4. Look at what Paul cautions them about in verse 5, and examine his thinking behind this in verses 3–4. What application does this caution have for you?

5. What were the Corinthians guilty of, based on what Paul writes in verses 6–7?

6. Review what Paul says about the apostles in verses 9–13. Why do you think God called them to provide the kind of example they did?

7. What kinds of changes do you think Paul wanted the Corinthian believers to make as a result of this instruction?

8. What can you learn from this passage?

SESSION 6

TEAM MINISTRY

For the Leader

Experiencing LeaderShift is a system. One of the primary reasons it's put together as a system is to help build teams. The book *Experiencing LeaderShift*, its companion *Application Guide,* and *Experiencing LeaderShift Together,* for ministry teams and small groups, are all written with an eye toward *team.*

You're a leader, which means you have a group of people following you. Whether this group numbers three, thirty, or three hundred, you face the challenge of building the individual members into a team. Foundational to accomplishing this objective is the need for common understanding about ministry, as well as a shared terminology for interaction.

It's our hope that as you reach this last session, your ministry team or small group will have made significant progress in developing a common understanding about ministry, as well as a common "language" for interacting with each other regarding ministry. Sharing these things is fundamental to functioning as a team.

We encourage you to continue using the *Experiencing LeaderShift* system to increase the common ground among all your current and future team members.

Objectives

One of the greatest challenges facing any leader is that of turning a group of individuals into a team. A group of people working *as individuals* will never accomplish as much as they would working *as a team.*

Once it does happen, you'll find that functioning as a true team has a way of vastly multiplying the joy each person feels in doing his or her own part.

For building a team, this session is intended to assist you in three specific ways:

1. To help everyone gain a vision for team, clearly understanding the difference between being a true team member and simply being an individual in a group.

2. To grow in the skills and understanding required for individuals to function as teammates.

3. For each person to desire this: "I want to be a member of a team, and I won't settle for anything less."

Icebreaker (optional; 5–8 minutes)

With a team focus in mind, identify an icebreaker that will enable the people in your group to connect with one another on a deeper level.

For example, have each person complete this sentence: "I could really use your prayer concerning …" or "I'm really struggling with …"

Prayer Together

If you followed the above icebreaker suggestion, pray for one another regarding the needs and requests that were shared. This will be well worth the time it takes.

You may also want to focus your prayer time on unity. In your own words, express to the Lord this desire: "Come, make us one. Give us the unity You want us to have."

Learning Together

Note to leader: **As elsewhere, this content is included in the Participant's Guide (starting on page 121)—except for text in bold (like this), which is for you as the leader.**

Introduction

Note to leader: **Have someone read this aloud.**

At school, at church, at work, or in the community, all of us have had opportunities for involvement in groups that are pursuing common tasks or goals. But how many true *teams* have you been on?

We intuitively know the difference, don't we? Group experiences are common; team experiences, not so much.

In this session, we want to look at the difference between a simple group and a true team. As we've seen already, we're called to function as the *body* of Christ—and such an analogy screams "Team!" Many members working together *as one*—that's God's will for us as we follow Him and participate as members of His family.

Team is something God models for us in His very nature as Father, Son, and Holy Spirit. The concept of the Trinity is difficult for us to get our minds around, but the truth is that God is three in one: one God, three members. God doesn't merely *want* team, He *is* team. He embodies team.

This is His will for us as His people. May your understanding of this truth become a conviction that causes you to settle for nothing less than a team experience as a member of the body of Christ. That's what *Experiencing LeaderShift Together*—and this session in particular—is all about.

Warm-Up Questions (10 minutes)

Can you think back on an experience with a group of people who became a "team" for you? What made this a team experience? In what ways was it different than other experiences you've had in working or participating with a group of people?

Note to leader: Draw forth from each member the feelings he or she associated with being on this team. As everyone in your group "feels" the difference between group participation and team membership, it will bring this session's content to life.

DVD Teaching (16 minutes)

Take notes as you watch and listen to the final DVD teaching segment in this study.

This session's teaching focuses on the following points:

1. There's a clear difference between participating in a group and belonging to a team.

2. God's desire is that we fully experience all that it means to be on a team. This is clearly seen in Paul's description of the body of Christ in 1 Corinthians 12.

3. There are characteristic differences between a group and a team (five of which are mentioned in the DVD).

4. Two criteria must be met to ensure a team experience for members:
   a) Each member must feel a sense of belonging.

   b) Each member must make a valued contribution to the work of the team.

5. To experience team, members must relate to one another as teammates. There are a number of ways to build teammate relationships.

6. God Himself dwells within a context of team. He is Father, Son, and Holy Spirit—three in one. This is *team*. We're created in God's image and therefore built with a longing for such a relationship with others.

Key Bible Passage

The following passages speak to the concept of team. Though we've covered these passages in previous sessions, they're worthy of another look.

Note to leader: **To briefly reinforce the biblical concept of team, you could have group members read aloud select verses from these passages.**

- Acts 2:42–47
- Romans 12:4–16
- 1 Corinthians 12:1–31 (emphasis on verses 12–27)
- Ephesians 4:1–6
- Philippians 2:1–5

Discussion (20–30 minutes)

Once again, your discussion of these questions is the most important part of the session.

1. What do you believe to be the primary characteristics of a team? List them as clearly as you can.

2. For what reasons do you believe God wants us to experience being part of a team? Why isn't it enough (from God's perspective) for us to simply participate as individuals in a group?

3. On a scale of 1 to 10, to what degree do you feel your current involvement in ministry is reflective of a team experience? (1 = I'm only an individual in a group; 10 = it's fully a team experience)

4. If your answer wasn't a "10" on the previous question, what do you think would help move your number higher? (Be specific.)

5. What could be done to increase the sense of belonging that currently exists among those you serve with? (Be specific.)

6. If it's true that *we must make a valued contribution* in order to feel we're truly on a team, what could be done to increase that aspect of your experience in serving with others?

7. As a result of being a part of this study, how has your team experience been enhanced as you serve in ministry with others?

For Ministry Teams

1. On a scale of 1 to 10, to what degree do you believe we function as a unified team rather than as individuals? (1 = primarily as individuals; 10 = fully as a team)

2. Review this list (from the DVD teaching) of ideas for becoming better teammates:
   —Pray with and for one another.
   —Increase the depth of conversation with one another.
   —Have shared experiences outside of ministry tasks.
   —Encourage one another.
   —Have fun with one another.
   —Dream together about the future of our ministry.
   —Spend time strategizing how we would be more effective in accomplishing our mission.
   —Celebrate what God is accomplishing in and through our team.
   —Thank God and worship Him together.
   From this list, identify two or three steps your members could take to improve your functioning as a team.

3. What could we do as a team to better assimilate new members as they come on board?

4. What can we do specifically in the weeks and months ahead to grow as a team?

5. What do we as a team want to gain from having completed *Experiencing LeaderShift Together?* (Make a list of specific actions steps.)

This would be a great time to pray together, asking for God's working in and through your team.

Application Zone

Scripture Memory

Be devoted to one another in brotherly love; give preference to one another in honor. (Rom. 12:10)

So that there may be no division in the body, but that the members may have the same care for one another. And if one member suffers, all the members suffer with it; if one member is honored, all the members rejoice with it. Now you are Christ's body, and individually members of it. (1 Cor. 12:25–27)

Being diligent to preserve the unity of the Spirit in the bond of peace. There is one body and one Spirit, just as also you were called in one hope of your calling; one Lord, one faith, one baptism, one God and Father of all who is over all and through all and in all. (Eph. 4:3–6)

Do nothing from selfishness or empty conceit, but with humility of mind regard one another as more important than yourselves; do not merely look out for your own personal interests, but also for the interests of others. (Phil. 2:3–4)

Daily Devotions

Day 1

Read and reflect on Mark 6:7–13.

[7] And He called the twelve to Himself, and began to send them out two by two, and gave them power over unclean spirits. [8] He commanded them to take nothing for the journey except a staff—no bag, no bread, no copper in their money belts— [9] but to wear sandals, and not to put on two tunics.

[10] Also He said to them, "In whatever place you enter a house, stay there till you depart from that place. [11] And whoever will not receive you nor hear you, when you depart from there, shake off the

dust under your feet as a testimony against them. Assuredly, I say to you, it will be more tolerable for Sodom and Gomorrah in the day of judgment than for that city!"

¹² So they went out and preached that people should repent. ¹³ And they cast out many demons, and anointed with oil many who were sick, and healed them. (Mark 6:7–13 NKJV)

1. When Jesus sends out the Twelve in ministry, He sends them in pairs (v. 7). Why is this significant?

2. Why is the giving of authority significant in any team enterprise (v. 7)?

3. What was Jesus doing with His team in verses 8–11? What application does this have for us today?

4. Make a list of all the specific instructions Jesus gives here to train His team members.

5. Review your list for question 4 and explain why each instruction was of value. What would these twelve men have gained or learned or received as a result of following Jesus' instructions?

6. What is the connection between what occurred in verses 12–13 and what you read in verse 7?

7. What can you learn and gain from the events of this passage?

Day 2

Read and reflect on these two gospel accounts of Jesus choosing His twelve apostles.

[12] Now it came to pass in those days that He went out to the mountain to pray, and continued all night in prayer to God. [13] And when it was day, He called His disciples to Himself; and from them He chose twelve whom He also named apostles: [14] Simon, whom He also named Peter, and Andrew his brother; James and John; Philip and Bartholomew; [15] Matthew and Thomas; James the son of Alphaeus, and Simon called the Zealot; [16] Judas the son of James, and Judas Iscariot who also became a traitor. (Luke 6:12–16 NKJV)

[13] And He went up on the mountain and called to Him those He Himself wanted. And they came to Him. [14] Then He appointed twelve, that they might be with Him and that He might send them out to preach, [15] and to have power to heal sicknesses and to cast out demons: [16] Simon, to whom He gave the name Peter; [17] James the son of Zebedee and John the brother of James, to whom He gave the name Boanerges, that is, "Sons of Thunder"; [18] Andrew, Philip, Bartholomew, Matthew, Thomas, James the son of Alphaeus, Thaddaeus, Simon the Cananite; [19] and Judas Iscariot, who also betrayed Him. And they went into a house. (Mark 3:13–19 NKJV)

1. According to Luke 6:12, what preceded Jesus' selection of these twelve men? Why do you think this is important?

2. According to Mark 3:14–15, what kinds of ministry were the twelve apostles originally called to?

3. What do these passages reveal to you about the team-building strategies and purposes that Jesus pursued?

Day 3

In your Bible, look up Acts 1:1–15 and 2:1–13. Here Jesus is passing on the baton of ministry to His followers. Read and reflect on these passages.

1. From this unfolding story, what evidence do you see that Jesus had built and led His team well?

2. What can you gain from this story, whether you're the leader of a team or a member of it? Make a list of the implications and applications for your life and ministry.

Day 4

Read and reflect on 2 Timothy 4:9–22.

[9] Be diligent to come to me quickly; [10] for Demas has forsaken me, having loved this present world, and has departed for Thessalonica—Crescens for Galatia, Titus for Dalmatia. [11] Only Luke is with me. Get Mark and bring him with you, for he is useful to me for ministry. [12] And Tychicus I have sent to Ephesus. [13] Bring the cloak that I left with Carpus at Troas when you come—and the books, especially the parchments.

[14] Alexander the coppersmith did me much harm. May the Lord repay him according to his works. [15] You also must beware of him, for he has greatly resisted our words.

[16] At my first defense no one stood with me, but all forsook me. May it not be charged against them.

[17] But the Lord stood with me and strengthened me, so that the message might be preached fully through me, and that all the Gentiles might hear. Also I was delivered out of the mouth of the lion. [18] And the Lord will deliver me from every evil work and preserve me for His heavenly kingdom. To Him be glory forever and ever. Amen!

[19] Greet Prisca and Aquila, and the household of Onesiphorus. [20] Erastus stayed in Corinth, but Trophimus I have left in Miletus sick.

²¹ Do your utmost to come before winter.

Eubulus greets you, as well as Pudens, Linus, Claudia, and all the brethren.

²² The Lord Jesus Christ be with your spirit. Grace be with you. Amen. (2 Tim. 4:9–22 NKJV)

Those are the last words, in the last chapter, of the last letter the apostle Paul wrote before his death.

1. What to you is most significant about this content?

2. Make a list of each person Paul names here, and the nature of that person's relationship with Paul as indicated in this passage.

3. Describe in your own words what Paul must have been thinking and feeling as he wrote these words.

4. What does this passage tell you about your relationship with other believers?

5. What will you do to apply what you've read and studied here? (Be specific and practical.)

Day 5

In your Bible, look up John 17:1–26, and read and reflect on this passage.

Here John records Jesus' conversation with His Father as His life and ministry on earth were nearing an end. A great deal can be gleaned from His prayer about His relationship with God the Father, as well as His desires for us, His followers.

Read this chapter slowly and reflectively as you carefully answer the following questions. (Plan to stretch this out over several days.)

1. Note every reference in this prayer to Jesus' relationship with His Father in heaven. What can you learn about Their relationship, based on Jesus' words here? Make a detailed list of your observations.

2. Note every reference Jesus makes here to us, His followers. What does each reference tell you about His thoughts and feelings toward us?

3. Make a list of every request Jesus makes on our behalf over the course of the prayer.

4. What implications for your life and ministry flow from what you've gleaned from Jesus' prayer?

ADDITIONAL RESOURCES

Printed Materials

Network

Bruce Bugbee and Don Cousins, Zondervan
- Leader's Guide
- Participant's Guide
- DVD Drama Vignettes
- CD PowerPoint, User's Guide, Coach's Guide

Available in Spanish and many other languages

What You Do Best in the Body of Christ

Bruce Bugbee, Zondervan

Available in Spanish and many other languages

Discover Your Spiritual Gifts the Network Way

Bruce Bugbee, Zondervan

Walking with God

Don Cousins and Judson Poling, Zondervan

Available in Spanish and many other languages

Here is how you can personally contact Don and Bruce:

Don Cousins—individual coaching, ministry
consulting, training, and speaking
www.doncousins.org
616-396-9625
don.cousins@sbcglobal.net

Bruce Bugbee & Associates—leadership
assessments, training, and ministry consulting
www.brucebugbee.com
800-588-8833
staff@brucebugbee.com

NOTES